THIRD-WORLD POLITICAL ORGANIZATIONS

THIRD-WORLD POLITICAL ORGANIZATIONS

A Review of Developments

Gwyneth Williams

First published 1981 by
THE MACMILLAN PRESS LTD
London and Basingstoke
Companies and representatives
throughout the world

ISBN 0 333 28202 7

Typeset and printed in Hong Kong

Contents

List of Tables

Abbreviations

ACP	African, Caribbean and Pacific States
ANCOM	Andean Common Market
ASEAN	Association of South-East Asian Nations
ASPAC	Asian and Pacific Council
CENTO	Central Treaty Organisation
CIEC	Conference on International Economic Cooperation
CMEA/COMECON	Council for Mutual Economic Assistance
dc	Developed country
ECA	Economic Commission for Africa
ECOSOC	Economic and Social Council
ECLA	Economic Commission for Latin America
EEC	European Economic Community
EPTA	Expanded Programme of Technical Assistance
FAO	Food and Agriculture Organisation
GATT	General Agreement on Trade and Tariffs
GNP	Gross National Product
GSP	Generalised System of Preferences
IBRD	International Bank for Reconstruction and Development
IFC	International Finance Corporation
ILO	International Labour Office
IMF	International Monetary Fund
ITO	International Trade Organisation
ldc	Less developed country
lldc	Least developed country
MFN	Most Favoured Nation
MSA	Most Seriously Affected Country
NIEO	New International Economic Order
OAS	Organisation of American States
OAU	Organisation of African Unity
OECD	Organisation for Economic Cooperation and Development

Abbreviations

OPEC	Organisation of Petroleum Exporting Countries
OTC	Organisation for Trade Cooperation
SDR	Special Drawing Rights
SEATO	South East Asia Treaty Organisation
UAM	Union Africaine et Malgache
UN	United Nations
UNCSAT	UN Conference on Science and Technology
UNCTAD	UN Conference of Trade and Development
UNDP	UN Development Programme
UNEP	UN Environment Programme
UNIDO	UN Industrial Development Organisation

Acknowledgements

Acknowledgement is gratefully made to all those people and institutions who have contributed to my interest and efforts. Particular thanks are expressed to those working at grass-roots level in the Third World with whom I have enjoyed the privilege of personal association; to colleagues at the Overseas Development Institute who provided me with an introduction to the complexities of underdevelopment; to Professor David Henderson who first stimulated my interest in the subject of this book; to Ann Weston for reading the manuscript; to colleagues at the BBC who provided encouragement; to friends who helped through many discussions and cups of tea; and to my father for his constant support.

Introduction

This book is concerned with one aspect of the Third World, its political organisations. But it is a crucial aspect in that it represents perhaps the best hope of success in achieving solutions to problems of underdevelopment.

Underdevelopment is an incredibly complex matter involving inter-related political, economic, social and cultural issues. While there may not be agreement as to its causes and solutions there does exist a general consensus regarding its characteristics and problems. These clearly relate to quality of life and to basic human rights; for a very large proportion of the world's people it is a matter of poverty and inequality. The attributes of underdevelopment are not those of a state of nature, but represent a process, a set of problems with causes and thus possible solutions.

Such characteristics provide enough common ground for one to talk of a Third World. But it is evident that the term is merely one of convenience. Every one of its countries is different: some are capitalist, some Communist; some agricultural, some mineral producers; some very poor, some not so poor; some oil producers, some oil exporters; some least developed, some developing. The list is endless.

Within each country again exist immense differences and divisions in so many respects. And when one is concerned with North–South dialogue — a term widely used to cover the whole area of negotiations and contact between the developed and underdeveloped world — what is meant is negotiation between their elites.

The book thus provides a summary review of the efforts of the Third World to organise politically, through what has become known as the North–South dialogue, in order to achieve what it regards as its rightful place in the world community. This is attempted by outlining the development, over the last few decades, of its major organisations and conferences; through these its aspirations have been pursued, its dilemmas exposed, and some successes achieved. The sequence is dealt with in some detail, but it is hoped that the major issues have remained clear.

The points of view of both the developed and less developed countries are put forward, but those of the latter are emphasised and interpreted as well as is possible by a writer not of the Third World. The approach is factual, but commentary and explanation is necessary and is provided through a 'realistic or objective subjectivity' which the writer considers essential in dealing with controversial issues.

The subject is an enormous one so that selection is clearly necessary, and even then a full treatment is not attempted; each topic considered lends itself to much further study and research. Thus the book is designed for a variety of readers. For the expert in the field it represents a convenient source of information on the sequence of events; for experts in other aspects of underdevelopment it seeks to assist in providing information on political issues; for the informed reader who is interested in one of the modern world's most important problems it presents a useful summary review of developments.

The book has been written out of concern for the Third World. It was prompted by personal experience of conditions in some of its countries, and encouraged by study and research in its affairs.

Certain organisations and conferences which seem to the writer to be most significant have been selected for presentation in chapter form, while others like the Group of 77 and the New International Economic Order have been considered *en passant* within several chapters as they become relevant. The topics of each chapter when considered together provide a composite picture; every one is highly complex in its own right, but what is far more important is that they are all interrelated.

The first two chapters deal with the United Nations Conferences on Trade and Development — UNCTAD I to V. These are followed by an account of the Non-aligned Movement, and the Sixth and Seventh Special Sessions of the United Nations General Assembly. The last two chapters discuss OPEC and the North–South Conference on International Economic Cooperation. Finally, as an Appendix at the end of the book is provided a Date Chart of the Main Events Affecting the Third World from 1944 to 1980, so that reference may be made — at any stage of reading — to the overall sequence of events considered in the previous chapters.

In this manner, in an order which seems reasonable but is by no means inflexible, an attempt is made to separate the interwoven threads of a highly complex subject, and at the same time to bring out their interrelationships.

1 UNCTAD I The First United Nations Conference on Trade and Development Geneva 1964

This conference was described by the Secretary-General of the UN, U Thant, as one of the most important events since the establishment of the United Nations.

The Third World had high hopes for UNCTAD, looking to it as paving the way towards the goal of economic emancipation from the neo-colonialism they saw implicit in the trade relationships then prevailing between rich and poor countries.

In the first place it provided a platform for Third World hopes and aspirations, and one that the ldcs had themselves created. In the second place it provided a framework for future debate on economic development, underlining the connections between aid and trade and focusing international attention upon improvement of the former and reform of the latter. Its major subject areas are as valid today as they were in 1964.

UNCTAD should really be seen as a charter of dissatisfactions and demands from the Third World. Its major achievements are not specific policy decisions, and they are not enforceable, but they led to a general change in North–South relationships and to the extension of these relationships into a crucial area of international concern.

HOW UNCTAD I CAME ABOUT

The initiative for UNCTAD I came from the Third World. In 1961 at

1

the sixteenth session of the United Nations General Assembly the less developed countries (ldcs) took this initiative in proposing a world trade conference to concentrate on their problems. Two draft resolutions (by the Latin American states, the African states and Indonesia) were introduced into the Second Committee of the UN calling for action in international trade and stressing the need for an international conference. The Latin American draft was amended to incorporate both, resubmitted, and then approved by eighty-one votes to none, with eleven abstentions — significantly from the major trading nations. The final resolution dealt with international trade as a primary instrument for economic development.

The upshot of this was that governments were consulted by the UN Secretary-General in 1962 as to their opinion of the advisability of such an international trade conference and of the topics that might be discussed. The result was that 45 nations proved to be in favour of the conference, 18 were indifferent or opposed to it, and 3 had no objections. In July 1962 36 ldcs met in Cairo at a conference on Problems of Developing Countries, and this led to the Cairo Declaration to the UN General Assembly which avowed itself to be 'resolutely in favour of the holding of an international economic conference within the framework of the UN'.[1]

With such pressure from the ldcs (as well as from the Soviet Union) it soon became clear that the USA and the West would have to accept an international conference. Finally, three days after the opening in 1962 of the 34th session of the Economic and Social Council (ECOSOC), Brazil, Ethiopia, India, Senegal and Yugoslavia submitted a draft resolution empowering the Council to recommend that the General Assembly should adopt a resolution convening a UN Conference on international trade problems in 1963. It was also recommended that the resolution should urge that the agenda of the conference include 'essential questions relating to international trade, international primary commodity markets and economic relations between the developing countries and the highly developed countries'. Western delegates were reluctant to commit themselves publicly; only the UK referred directly to the proposed conference and then to assert that little was likely to be accomplished.

The matter was then referred to the Economic Committee of the Council, and on 26 July the sponsors of the draft submitted a revised text:[2] UNCTAD was to be convened by the Council and not by the General Assembly; the year for the conference was not specified; a preparatory committee of experts designated by governments who were members of ECOSOC should convene in early 1963 to consider the agenda for the conference; the Secretary-General was to be asked to prepare (with the help of the Food and Agriculture Organisation (FAO), the International Monetary Fund (IMF), the General Agreement on Trade and Tariffs (GATT), the International Bank for Reconstruction and Development (IBRD or World Bank), regional economic councils and others) appropriate documentation and proposals for the conference, for consideration by the Preparatory Committee; the Preparatory Committee was to report to ECOSOC at its 63rd summer session.

On 31 July after discussion in the Economic Committee of the Council consensus was reached. This led to the draft resolution being approved unanimously, and ECOSOC adopted it on 3 August 1962. The decision to convene UNCTAD had been formally taken.[3]

This decision was clearly the result of Third World initiative, but the long-term sequence of events which led to it requires consideration and understanding, since the history of UNCTAD I is inextricably bound up with that of Third World political development. Certain of the many relevant issues — which are broad, complex and indeed interrelated — are now summarily considered in varying degrees of detail, and in some cases elaborated upon in later chapters: non-alignment, African independence, GATT, contemporary international relations, commodity agreements, the UN Development Decade, ldc economic problems.

Non-alignment
This movement is particularly important since it marks the beginning of ldc consciousness of common needs and problems, and an awareness of greater strength in collective action. As the movement developed economic issues were increasingly recognised as important and these were reflected in the second non-aligned summit of 1964 in Cairo which concentrated particularly on economic development. The non-aligned group by then had grown in number from 25 members at Belgrade to 47. UNCTAD I, providing a wider focus on the particular trade problems of ldcs, seemed to be a logical extension of the non-aligned group's discussions. The following events are of particular significance — the Asian–African Conference and the Bandung Declaration of 1955, the first summit of non-aligned countries at Belgrade in 1961, the Cairo Conference on Problems of Developing

Countries and the Cairo Declaration of 1962, the second summit of non-aligned countries at Cairo in 1964 — but a more detailed treatment of the movement is deferred to a later chapter.

African Independence
Another basic reason for the changes that led to UNCTAD I is to be found in the changing physical composition of the UN, brought about by newly independent states joining that organisation. From January 1960 to January 1965 alone over 25 African colonies gained independence, thus swelling the UN and fundamentally altering it. Perhaps more than any other event this changed the focus of the international community towards the problems of ldcs.

Developed country (dc) reaction to this change was also extremely important in relation to the attitudes of the Group of 77 and the Third World. The ldcs saw the initial dc reaction to them as one of mockery, and when later demands for changes grew, as one of hostility as the ldcs' majority became so large. This is reflected in the dispute over voting in UNCTAD I during which the dcs attempted to obtain some kind of weighted voting to compensate them for their numerical weakness.

The General Agreement on Trade and Tariffs (GATT)
GATT was most important in bringing about UNCTAD I largely because of a growing ldc disillusionment with it. While several events are particularly significant in this context[4] this disillusionment may be attributed to two main causes:

GATT's inadequacy as an institution for dealing with ldc trade problems
Part of UNCTAD's *raison d'être* was undoubtedly the strong feeling that there was no established organisation to focus on ldc trade problems and the problems of underdevelopment in general. This was never GATT's function. The Agreement was signed by 32 countries as a temporary measure to make a start in negotiating tariff reductions until the Havana Charter came into operation. The vital (to ldcs) Chapter 6 commodity agreements, and the eight articles concerned with development questions were not included in GATT. The contracting parties sought to provide 'not an institution at all but simply the contractual framework in which to incorporate the extensive tariff reductions and bindings that were negotiated in 1947 at Geneva'.[5] The organisation designed to fill the gap, the International Trade Organ-

isation (ITO) as envisaged by the Havana Charter did not come into being. The Havana Charter was negotiated under ECOSOC for the establishment of the ITO, but it was never ratified by the US Congress which criticised the Charter as a codification of malpractices and on the grounds that foreign economic planning violated fundamental US principles. This reaction influenced the UK not to recommend the ratification of the Charter to its Parliament.

Thus the gap which was to have been filled by the ITO was instead filled haphazardly since there was no comparable coordinating agency or common forum like it. In 1963, for instance, just before UNCTAD I, no less than 43 international organisations and sub-organisations dealing with commodity and trade problems had sprung into being, according to a report in that year — 'Not only is their number large but the rate of proliferation has been quite high ... there is an apprehension that, unless suitable countervailing measures are taken now, the number may go up much further during the next decade'.[6]

Some attempts were made to fill this gap in international organisation and eventually GATT itself in 1954–5 agreed to establish the Organisation for Trade Cooperation to administer GATT; but this was not ratified by the US Congress and did not come into existence.

Thus while criticism of GATT was rife, it was widely recognised by ldcs that as an institution it was not really equipped for a much wider role in trade and development. It was partly for this reason that a conference on these issues (UNCTAD I) was sought to consider changes that could be made.

GATT's bias against the Third World

Since its inception in 1947 GATT had been pre-occupied with trade between the dcs and it took a long time for it to become aware of the ldcs' pressing trade and development problems — too long in the view of most ldcs.

Certain positive changes however began to be effective in the early 1960s following the so-called Haberler Report of 1958,[7] and by 1964 the dcs were arguing that GATT could no longer be regarded as a 'rich man's club' since there were now twice as many ldcs as dcs party to the Agreement. One lasting and major advantage of GATT's changes, and a step towards UNCTAD I, was indeed the conceptual link that had now gradually but definitely been made between trade and development.

Nevertheless most ldcs still did not consider that GATT had really sufficiently departed from its concern with dcs and, although some

changes had occurred, they felt these were really the result of ldc
pressures to hold UNCTAD and to put those dcs not in favour of a
new institution in a better bargaining position at the proposed conference. In fact the Organisation for Economic Cooperation and Development (OECD) group had agreed that it would be easier to defend
GATT in UNCTAD if 'a certain number of concrete results in the
near future for developing nations' were produced.[8] Ldcs felt that
GATT had been shaped by dc interests and that the application of the
most favoured nation (MFN) choice was only possible with reciprocal
advantages if all countries had equal bargaining power. In the words
of an ldc delegate to GATT 'Equality of treatment is equitable only
among equals'.[9]

Membership of GATT was also a matter of dispute. Ldcs emphasised the problems involved in having to make concessions on joining, to
compensate for all the concessions negotiated before its accession.
Also, because tariffs were seen by GATT as the main tool in international policy the centrally-planned economies had remained outside
GATT. Thus opportunities for negotiating trade with these countries
were lost. Furthermore many ldcs were themselves organised on a centrally-planned basis, so they felt discriminated against.

Ldcs criticised GATT for having no special provisions regarding
international trade in primary commodities; and when changes were
contemplated they were often seen by ldcs as a direct response to dc
needs. In 1961 for instance GATT considered setting up a body to
concentrate on opening up markets for ldc exports. The reason for
this was suggested as being because GATT considered they might ease
the UK's EEC negotiations which were complicated by the need to
secure markets for Commonwealth produce.[10]

One of the ldcs' main concerns in the early 1960s was the formation
of dc regional groupings, particularly the EEC, and the implications
these would have on the trade of ldcs. For instance Pakistan's agenda
for UNCTAD itemed discussions on the worsening terms of ldc trade
in this context.[11] Some ldcs saw GATT as a useful body through which
to exert pressure on the EEC to keep external tariffs down, so that at
this time many of them felt loath to disrupt it; but it became increasingly obvious that the EEC was strong enough to resist many
pressures. Furthermore it caused a split between ldcs over the EEC's
special treatment of its 18 Associated Overseas Territories. Ldcs urged
that GATT should be more flexible in its attitude towards the formation of their own economic groupings.

Ldcs on the whole were sceptical about the outcome of the

'Kennedy Round' considering that previous efforts had, from their point of view, failed.[12] Nevertheless some were more hopeful about these talks, and the so-called 'moderate' group in UNCTAD argued that ldcs should aim to take as much advantage of the negotiations as possible. The strength of the feeling of disillusionment with GATT varied. Some countries like India, Pakistan, Malaysia, the United Arab Republic and many Latin American countries, which had long been GATT members felt less hostile towards the agreement. But by the early 1960s even those who had defended GATT in 1955 were beginning to have serious doubts about the wisdom of continuing to do so. Thus it can be seen that by 1964 many ldcs claimed the revisions introduced by GATT seemed 'like minor patching operations', and felt that the time had come to 're-examine from the very foundations upwards the whole structure of ideas which found their legal and constitutional expression in the GATT'.[13] At the same time it was also clear that the Soviet Union wished to replace GATT for political and economic reasons as discussed below.

Contemporary international relations

Undoubtedly the international climate had to be conducive to the convening of UNCTAD I, particularly in terms of the relationships of the great powers and the East–West conflict.

In the 1950s, long before UNCTAD, the Soviet Union had been pressing for a UN World Trade Conference in order to try to attack Western strategic trade controls as well as the US policy of denying the most favoured nation (MFN) treatment to the Soviet bloc; such a conference would provide a forum from which to attack the West. This goes some way to account for the initial US coldness towards UNCTAD.

In 1954 the USSR made its first call for an international conference of trade experts, and began advocating an international trade organisation with a universal membership. In 1955 the socialist countries introduced a draft resolution calling for the ratification of the Havana Charter which had been negotiated at the 1948 Conference for International Trade and Employment. In 1956 the USSR proposed a world economic conference to consider the establishment of a world trade organisation within the UN, but there was not sufficient support for this initiative since many ldcs were not prepared to support a conference focusing on East–West trade. Indeed, at the same Assembly session a resolution was adopted which stressed that the existing international organisations and agreements provided a basis for discussion of trade problems.[14] In 1958 the USSR proposed in ECOSOC's 26th Session that a new UN Conference on Trade and Employment be convened to create an international trade organisation based on the Organisation for Trade Cooperation (OTC) model. Thereafter it continued to support the holding of UNCTAD, and later to argue at UNCTAD for the forming of a new institution to deal with world trade.

By the early 1960s a major change was taking place — the Cold War was becoming more of an accepted fact, so that the situation was sufficiently fluid for the Third World to emerge as a new force. 'For the first time since 1946 the Cold War was drowned out by the insistent economic demands of the 75 developing countries.'[15] At the same time Soviet and US hostility continued, and the economic and political dependence of the Third World seemed to be an effective way of gaining influence. International relations were at a flexible stage and the Third World was able to use this situation successfully to focus attention on its trade problems. The ldcs thus seized the initiative for holding a world trade conference in 1961, and managed to get UNCTAD I convened on their own terms, defeating the Soviet Union's aims and those of the US, which in the light of Third World demands finally came round to accepting it.

The Soviet Union did not really play a major part in the conference, which developed into a confrontation between the West and the ldcs. However it was able, by voting consistently with the ldcs, to show where its sympathies lay and to win the gratitude of some of them. This attitude contrasted with that of the Americans which was particularly tough under their negotiator, and made the USA even more unpopular at UNCTAD I than it was already for its leadership of the West.

Predictably, when the institutional question was raised towards the end of UNCTAD I, the Soviet Union put forward the most forceful agruments in support of a new independent body. The ldcs criticised GATT and most of them also called for new institutional arrangements. The West on the other hand argued that there was no point in forming new institutions until their detailed objectives had been defined and the conference was satisfied that the existing machinery was inadequate.

With its support for ldc proposals, the Soviet Union was also called on to take positive action towards the Third World as regards aid and trade. The ldcs were keen to increase their exports into the Soviet bloc, with which their trade thus far had been very small. Imports by the

Soviet bloc from ldcs amounted to about £1 billion (UK) compared
with £19 billion by the dcs. A major cause of this was the Soviet bloc's
insistence on bilateral balancing of accounts, by which ldcs received
the right to choose an equivalent value of Soviet goods. The USSR
claimed that such long-term bilateral agreements offered stability to
ldc trade, but available data showed fluctuations in Soviet bloc pur-
chases, and many ldcs sought a change.

Thus despite the all-pervading nature of super-power politics,
UNCTAD I was held, and concentrated on issues important to ldcs.
By that time the East–West conflict was largely in abeyance and this
helped to confirm the break-up of the previous bi-polar division of the
world during the Cold War.

Commodity agreements
Another factor which undoubtedly contributed to a growing awareness of ldc trade problems was the increasing number of commodity
agreements signed in the few years before UNCTAD I. It seems likely
that this was an incentive to the holding of the conference. Ldc
difficulties in this area were certainly one of the main issues at
UNCTAD I, and since then action on commodities has been central to
UNCTAD's programme. Since 1974 the UNCTAD Secretariat has
been attempting to construct an 'integrated programme' for commodities in order to combine fair terms of trade for exporting ldcs
with secure access to supplies for importing countries.

As early as August 1950 ECOSOC authorised the Secretary-General
of the UN to commence intergovernmental conferences on specific
commodity problems. A year later on 21 December 1951 the Commonwealth Sugar Agreement was signed; this was an eight-year agreement embodying a contract by the exporting parties to supply and by
the UK Ministry of Agriculture to buy agreed quantities of sugar each
year at fixed prices. The first International Sugar Agreement was
signed on 1 January 1954 under the auspices of the UN, and similarly
in 1956 the first International Wheat Agreement which was renewed in
1959 and again in 1962. On 1 July 1956 the UN arranged the International Tin Agreement; UNCTAD was later to provide the forum for
these negotiations, and the Second Agreement was signed in 1962. The
UN Conference on Lead and Zinc was held at Geneva in 1958.

In 1958 at Montreal the Commonwealth Economic Conference considered the subject of commodity stabilisation, since commodities
were badly hit at that time by the US recession. At this conference
Britain was much more prepared to consider accepting new obliga-

tions as a banker to the rest of the Commonwealth than it was to initiate schemes of commodity stabilisation. The arguments on the issue at the conference reflected very divergent views by dc and ldc countries.[16]

In June 1959 an International Agreement on Olive Oil was signed at the UN, and in 1963 the International Coffee Agreement.

In its 1962 Report the Interim Committee for International Commodity Arrangements, which was set up under ECOSOC, warned of possible difficulties in operating international commodity agreements because of what it described as 'sheltered' regional trading groups.

Gradually, as both dcs and ldcs became aware of the political as well as the economic importance of commodity trade, the issue became more and more central in North–South negotiations. Growing recognition of the importance of ldcs as primary commodity producers must have considerably increased their demands for UNCTAD I.

The United Nations development decade

On 19 December 1961 the General Assembly decided unanimously on a proposal originally put forward by the American President of the time, John F. Kennedy, that the 1960s would be designated a UN Development Decade. At the same time the Second Committee accepted a resolution which provided that the Secretary-General should consult with UN governments on the advisability of holding UNCTAD I, and on the topics to be discussed; the resolution was entitled 'International trade as a primary instrument for economic development'.

The terms of the UN development decade were: ldcs should attain a minimum annual growth rate in aggregate national income of 5 per cent or more during the 1960s; the General Assembly reaffirmed its aim of increasing the annual flow of international assistance and capital to the ldcs to 1 per cent of the combined national incomes of dcs; the UN recognised that international trade had a key role to play in effecting crucial changes in the economic structures of ldcs.

International acceptance of this was of fundamental importance, and certainly helped create the right climate for UNCTAD I. Until then the whole concept of national economic development plans was far from widely accepted; indeed until the Kennedy Administration such plans were often considered by the American establishment to be subversive. It now became necessary to think in terms of joint responsibilities and coordinated efforts through international organisations. The endorsement of the development decade marked a shift towards multilateral action by the dcs, although it may also have been seen as an extension of their influence in the Third World. It was certainly a response to increasing Third World politicisation, and there is no doubt that it helped to confirm recognition of the link between aid and trade in development, and thus was a step towards UNCTAD. As the Pakistan newspaper *Dawn* commented 'the convening of UNCTAD is a logical corollary to the World Organisation's decision to declare the 1960s to be the Development Decade. A 5 per cent minimum annual rate of growth for ldcs is attainable within the framework of the present pattern of international trade, so the basic aim of UNCTAD is to remove this basic incompatibility between the Development Decade target and the climate of World Trade.'[17]

Ldc economic problems
Underlying all other reasons for UNCTAD I lies the poverty of the Third World. The ldcs face great economic difficulties in their efforts to achieve a satisfactory level of economic development. These problems are seen by them as not of their making, and capable of resolution only through concerted world action. Thus the fervour of ldcs for UNCTAD can be attributed to a sense of injustice with which their leadership is fired.

During the 1950s the ldcs' needs to import were increasing, while their export earnings and capacity to import what they needed were inadequate. Furthermore they had growing debt service payments. At the same time the terms of trade for ldc exports (mostly primary commodities) were worsening, while the prices of their imports were rising. Ldcs failed to attain a high rate of export expansion largely because they exchanged primary goods for manufactures; the former expanded slowly for various reasons such as growing output in dcs (insulated by agricultural protection), the use of synthetics and substitutes and the slow increase in food demand from dcs. The prices of their commodities declined after the Korean War and this in turn helped bring about an ldc deficit in 1962 of £2.3 billion (UK).[18] Ldcs were frustrated in their attempts to increase manufactured and semi-manufactured products by dc tariff and non-tariff barriers.

The ideology underlying UNCTAD seemed to have been based on the feeling that modern trade, founded on classical economic theory, carries with it an essentially static view of the world. It assumes the existing distribution of resources among countries. Thus by pursuing liberal and non-discriminatory trade policies each country is encouraged to concentrate on the areas of its greatest comparative advantage. But treating all countries alike perpetuates the existing unequal patterns of production in the world. And the whole point of development is to remedy this inequality. This is part of the reason why even the Kennedy Round was rejected out of hand by some ldcs because it was seen as part of an old, inequitable and unfair system.

Despite all this the ldcs recognised that they had to concentrate on improving their position as primary producers in the short run, because this was all they were able to do. And this meant unstable foreign exchange earnings and slow growth in demand for exports over the longer run. They recognised that long-term security demanded basic changes in their production patterns, but they felt they could not achieve these alone.

Thus UNCTAD was considered vitally important to the Third World — an essential forum at which to focus attention on its problems and begin to change things towards a new order as yet unenunciated but already in motion.

GROUP POSITIONS IN UNCTAD I

UNCTAD member states fall into several groups, not all of which are mutually exclusive: The Group of 77; Groups A, B, C, D; the last four are the official groups of UNCTAD. These are now discussed. Their member states are listed in Tables 1.1, 1.2, 1.3, 1.4, 1.5, and OECD member states in Table 1.6.

One feature that emerged in UNCTAD I and was peculiar to it at the time was the group system of negotiating. This arose from the polarisation between ldcs and dcs, and from their disparity in bargaining power. It was initiated by the ldcs who felt that the only weapon they had against the more powerful developed market economies was their strength in unity.[19] This necessitated agreement within a group before negotiations could take place, but it also provoked similar group reaction from the dcs.

The group of 77
(Table 1.1 Ldcs. An unofficial but very influential group in which Group A and C tend to join together)

The Joint Declaration of the Group of 77 was issued at the end of UNCTAD I. It read: 'The unity [of the developing countries in UNCTAD] has sprung out of the fact that facing the basic problems of development they have a common interest in a new policy for inter-

TABLE 1.1
The Group of 77 ldcs member states 1979

13

Afghanistan	Guinea-Bissau	Qatar
Algeria	Guyana	Republic of Korea
Angola	Haiti	Rumania
Argentina	Honduras	Rwanda
Bahamas	India	Samoa
Bahrain	Indonesia	Sao Tome and
Bangladesh	Iran	Principe
Barbados	Iraq	Saudi Arabia
Benin	Ivory Coast	Senegal
Bhutan	Jamaica	Seychelles
Bolivia	Jordan	Sierra Leone
Botswana	Kenya	Singapore
Brazil	Kuwait	Solomon Islands
Burma	Lao People's	Somalia
Burundi	Democratic	South West African
Cape Verde	Republic	People's
Central African	Lebanon	Organisation
Empire	Lesotho	(SWAPO)
Chad	Liberia	Sri Lanka
Chile	Libyan Arab	Sudan
Colombia	Jamahiriya	Surinam
Comoros	Madagascar	Swaziland
Congo	Malawai	Syrian Arab Republic
Costa Rica	Malaysia	Thailand
Cuba	Maldives	Togo
Cyprus	Mali	Tonga
Democratic	Malta	Trinidad and Tobago
Kampuchea	Mauritania	Tunisia
Democratic People's	Mauritius	Uganda
Republic of Korea	Mexico	United Arab Emirates
Democratic Yemen	Mongolia	United Republic of
Djibouti	Morocco	Cameroon
Dominica	Mozambique	United Republic of
Dominican Republic	Nepal	Tanzania
Ecuador	Nicaragua	Upper Volta
Egypt	Niger	Uruguay
El Salvador	Nigeria	Venezuela
Equatorial Guinea	Oman	Vietnam (Socialist
Ethiopia	Pakistan	Republic of)
Fiji	Palestine Liberation	Yemen
Gabon	Organisation	Yugoslavia
Gambia	Panama	Zaire
Ghana	Papua New Guinea	Zambia
Grenada	Paraguay	Zimbabwean Patriotic
Guatemala	Peru	Front
Guinea	Philippines	

SOURCE: UN document TD/268, 13.7.1979.

TABLE 1.2
Group A ldcs member states 1979

Afghanistan	Iran	Rwanda
Algeria	Iraq	Samoa
Angola	Israel	Sao Tome and
Bahrain	Ivory Coast	Principe
Bangladesh	Jordan	Saudi Arabia
Benin	Kenya	Senegal
Bhutan	Kuwait	Seychelles
Botswana	Lao People's	Sierra Leone
Burma	Democratic	Singapore
Burundi	Republic	Solomon Islands
Cape Verde	Lebanon	Somalia
Central African	Lesotho	South Africa
Empire	Liberia	Sri Lanka
Chad	Libyan Arab	Sudan
China	Jamahiriya	Swaziland
Comoros	Madagascar	Syrian Arab Republic
Congo	Malawi	Thailand
Democratic	Malaysia	Togo
Kampuchea	Maldives	Tonga
Democratic People's	Mali	Tunisia
Republic of Korea	Mauritania	Uganda
Democratic Yemen	Mauritius	United Arab Emirates
Djibouti	Mongolia	United Republic of
Egypt	Morocco	Cameroon
Equatorial Guinea	Mozambique	United Republic of
Ethiopia	Nepal	Tanzania
Fiji	Niger	Upper Volta
Gabon	Nigeria	Vietnam (Socialist
Gambia	Oman	Republic of)
Ghana	Pakistan	Yemen
Guinea	Papua New Guinea	Yugoslavia
Guinea-Bissau	Philippines	Zaire
India	Qatar	Zambia
Indonesia	Republic of Korea	

SOURCE: UN document TD/268, 13.7.1979.

TABLE 1.3
Group B dcs member states 1979

Australia	Luxembourg
Austria	Malta
Belgium	Monaco
Canada	Netherlands
Cyprus	New Zealand
Denmark	Norway
Finland	Portugal
France	San Marino
Germany, Federal Republic of	Spain
Greece	Sweden
Holy See	Switzerland
Iceland	Turkey
Ireland	United Kingdom of Great Britain and
Italy	Northern Ireland
Japan	United States of America
Liechtenstein	

SOURCE: UN document TD/268, 13.7.1979.

TABLE 1.4
Group C member states Latin American countries 1979

Argentina	Guatemala
Bahamas	Guyana
Barbados	Haiti
Bolivia	Honduras
Brazil	Jamaica
Chile	Mexico
Colombia	Nicaragua
Costa Rica	Panama
Cuba	Paraguay
Dominica	Peru
Dominican Republic	Surinam
Ecuador	Trinidad and Tobago
El Salvador	Uruguay
Grenada	Venezuela

SOURCE: UN document TD/268, 13.7.1979.

TABLE 1.5
Group D member states Eastern bloc countries 1979

Albania	Hungary
Bulgaria	Poland
Byelorussian Soviet Socialist	Rumania
Republic	Ukrainian Soviet Socialist Republic
Czechoslovakia	Union of Soviet Socialist Republics
German Democratic Republic	

SOURCE: UN document TD/268, 13.7.1979.

TABLE 1.6
OECD member states 1979

Australia	Japan
Austria	Luxembourg
Belgium	Netherlands
Canada	New Zealand
Denmark	Norway
Finland	Portugal
France	Spain
Federal Republic of Germany	Sweden
Greece	Switzerland
Iceland	Turkey
Ireland	United Kingdom
Italy	United States of America

Yugoslavia participates in the work of the OECD with a special status

SOURCE: The Europa Yearbook, 1979.

national trade and development. The developing countries have a strong conviction that there is a vital need to maintain, and further strengthen, this unity in the years ahead. It is an indispensable instrument for securing the adoption of new attitudes and new approaches in the international economic field.'[20] The Declaration reflected the way the 77 ldcs had voted together in UNCTAD I, displaying a solidarity which was constantly discussed and commented on throughout the conference. The Group was born as an *ad hoc* group of co-sponsors of the 1963 Declaration, but developed at UNCTAD I into a permanent instrument to articulate ldc demands and improve negotiating capacity.

The 77 are characterised by their lack of institutional organisation, but the regional groups within them tend to be more institutionalised e.g. the Latin American group which possessed a rudimentary organisation as long ago as 1946. The leadership of the 77 also tends to be regionalised: in Latin America, Brazil and Chile; in Asia, India, Pakistan, the Philippines; and in Africa, Nigeria, Ghana, Algeria and the UAR. The three regional groups are:

The Latin American group
The Economic Commission for Latin America (ECLA) plays a central role in organising this group. It tended to deal with technical and economic matters for UNCTAD's agenda, and established the technical base for intergovernmental coordination in the Special Committee on Latin American Coordination. This was created just before UNCTAD in order to coordinate policies without the presence of the USA and Cuba. The ECLA was greatly helped in its task by possessing a common language, close historical, cultural and economic ties, and some experience of working together.

The African group
This really consisted of the Economic Commission for Africa (ECA), joint meetings of the ECA Working Party on Intra-African Trade, and the *ad hoc* committee of 14 of the Organisation of African Unity. This group undertook to formulate concrete proposals and recommendations on issues of interest to Africans. It has a far less cohesive nature than that of the Latin Americans and often has interest clashes as well as language problems.

The Asian group
This the least homogeneous of the three in all respects. The Economic

Commission for Asia and the Far East has not really been established as a coordinating body, partly because not all of the 77 belong to it, and partly because of the dc presence in it. The Group of 77 can be differentiated in several other ways. Perhaps the three most significant are:

(a) *Political and ideological differences*
In 1964 it was generally recognised that it would be impossible to reconcile the 77 politically. Thus there was a tacit understanding that many differences should be glossed over, and purely political matters were seldom discussed by the group. Political differences among them were certainly considerable, but these are probably best observed among the non-aligned states and in the General Assembly. The Group of 77 thus concentrated on economic matters where they had much in common. In UNCTAD I two main factions emerged within the Group of 77:
    (i) The Moderates e.g. India, Pakistan, Malaysia, the Philippines, and occasionally the UAR and many Latin American states; India played a particularly dominant role. Their policy was to try to avoid acrimonious confrontation between dcs and ldcs, and towards the end of the conference they sought to secure some reconciliation of views in the hope of dc concessions, realising that the efficacy of any new measures depended on Western cooperation.
    (ii) The Radicals e.g. Burma, Ghana, Indonesia. These were increasing numerically and pushed through many resolutions by their majority. They pressed for a new international trade organisation to supersede GATT, but with little regard for the readiness of the West to participate in it.
    At different times in the conference different groups set the pace. It was the moderate group, concerned to preserve possible ldc gains in the Kennedy Round, and to save UNCTAD I from collapse through conciliation with the dcs, which triumphed at the end, after the radicals failed to reach agreement in the final desperate negotiations to reach a consensus to conclude the conference.

(b) *Differences between the more developed and the less developed ldcs*
Not all ldcs are equally poor. One method of classification[21] differentiates between them as follows: higher income ldcs, middle income ldcs, poorest ldcs, most seriously affected countries (MSAs), least developed countries (lldcs). Sometimes alliances were forged among

the least developed countries to add to their bargaining power within the 77. Furthermore a country might be regarded as least developed if this suited the issue being considered e.g. Guatemala in 1965 was considered a least developed country by Latin America. Owing to the fact that UNCTAD opts to designate least developed countries for each item under consideration, some sort of selective coalition policy is more likely rather than a general confrontation between the least developed countries and the others, although the latter situation could arise.

(c) *Differences which result from links with dcs*
These are recognised as potentially the most damaging to the 77 since they present a dilemma between short-term interests (which can often be served by cooperation with a dc) and long-term development interests for which the unity of the 77 is recognised as dominant. The best example of this conflict can be seen in the case of those ldcs which in 1964 were EEC associates or members of the Commonwealth. It was tacitly understood that these would not attack each other over the issue of special preferences, but this provoked a conflict with the Latin Americans.

During the course of UNCTAD I two rules of behaviour came to apply to the 77: that all proposals had to be agreed by the Group of 77 before they were negotiated with the dcs, and that all proposals had to be unanimously endorsed by all Group members. As a result the ldcs exhibited at UNCTAD 1 a monolithic appearance which was seen by observers as transient and sustained by rhetoric. It was encouraged by the atmosphere of confrontation and by the endeavour to enunciate dissatisfactions and demands in forceful terms and was further consolidated by the negative attitude towards change adopted by Group B (discussed below).

Nevertheless when the permanent machinery of UNCTAD was established, the Group adhered to this method of in-group decision-making. Unity was considered paramount, as the only weapon possessed by the ldcs — to quote UNCTAD I's Secretary-General, Raul Prebisch, 'Whatever may divide the 77 it will always be far outweighed by what are the permanent economic common denominators uniting them.'[22] One of the problems of this method of negotiating was that agreement tended to be reached at the highest level of demand. This unfortunately conflicted with Group B's decisions, which tended to be reached around the area of minimum concession.

Group B
(Table 1.3   The Western developed countries)

The West had consulted on economic problems for some time, first in the EEC and then in the OECD. An OECD meeting was held before UNCTAD I to discuss the conference and try to establish loose and consultative guidelines. It was generally agreed that institutional change would be opposed as far as possible, and that the merits of GATT would be urged upon the conference. However at the conference, because of general polarisation and the attitude of the Group of 77, Group B began to assume a more rigid position. After UNCTAD the B Group became formally institutionalised, and a special ministerial decision was taken to have the OECD serve as its instrument.

Decision-making in Group B begins within the OECD where a general policy is adopted, and on this basis the group adjusts its position to changes that arise. But when an important issue is involved (e.g. preferences) and when the OECD decision is in the form of a package deal among dcs, the changes in negotiations can only be marginal and tactical.

Group B is smaller than the Group of 77, so decision-making is easier, while personalities tend to be less important. At the initial period of polarisation in UNCTAD I, the dcs were turning down ldc demands without incurring significant costs. But once this tactical stage passed and real dialogue began, Group B's decision-making became more complex. In the end interaction among the biggest trading nations tends to determine the group's position. This is the problem that leads to the resolution of Group B conflicts through the minimum common denominator, compared with the Group of 77 which resolves at the maximum. This is because in Group B the most powerful members are usually at the negative end. The US, France and the UK carry great influence together with a veto power, although halfway solutions can be attained without these powers e.g. the US and the EEC were not party to the sugar agreement. Special skills and interests, e.g. of Norway in shipping, also carry weight and provide leadership when these matters arise. The system of balances, which ensures the solidarity of group members on specific issues — the give and take of support — is also significant in Group B; e.g. the US supported maritime nations on shipping, although it was prepared to be relatively progressive towards the ldcs on this issue with the tacit understanding that these countries would not prove troublesome to the US over the question of aid.

As in the Group of 77, divisions within Group B are many, and include differences in level of development; differences between the EEC and the rest, with France and USA as prime examples of each; differences in attitudes towards the ldcs ranging from the view that more should be done for them (as held by the Netherlands and Sweden) to the view that dc prosperity should be maintained.

Group D
(Table 1.5   The Eastern bloc countries of Europe)

The Communist countries have always acted as a tightly knit group, using the CMEA as an organisational focus with its secretariat providing services. The political discipline common to the Eastern bloc was not always reflected over economic issues, e.g. Rumania often voted with the Group of 77 at UNCTAD when Group D did not, and since 1964 has claimed a place in that Group. Group D was characterised in UNCTAD I by its support for ldc demands and for a new international trade organisation. However proceedings at UNCTAD I were dominated by the 77 and Group B. (*Group A* (Table 1.2: Ldcs) and most of *Group C* (Table 1.4: Latin American countries) are considered under the Group of 77.)

CENTRAL ISSUES IN UNCTAD I

The Preparatory Committee of UNCTAD submitted its draft agenda which was approved by ECOSOC in 1963, and at the close of its second session an important declaration by ldcs was included in its report. This stressed the need for the conference to agree 'on a new international trade and development policy' which would involve improving the present institutional arrangements.[23]

In terms of the report five committees were set up at UNCTAD I to consider the following: international commodity problems; trade in manufactures and semi-manufactures; the improvement of invisible trade of ldcs, and the financing for an expansion of international trade; institutional arrangements, methods and machinery to implement measures relating to the expansion of international trade; expansion of international trade, its significance for economic development and the implications of regional economic groups.

The four central issues of the conference are now briefly discussed.

The institutional issue
The report of the Secretary-General, Raul Prebisch, was an important influence on this. Entitled 'Towards a new trade policy for development', it praised GATT for introducing the concept of the rule of law into world trade, argued that the tariff reductions negotiated mainly benefited the dcs and concluded by suggesting that some kind of new trade organisation was necessary and that the UN was capable of assuming greater responsibilities in this area.

A draft recommendation submitted to the fourth Committee by Burma, Ghana, Indonesia, Nigeria and Syria suggested the establishment of the conference as a permanent organ of the Assembly under Article 22 of the UN Charter, while the Latin Americans circulated their own draft recommendations calling for the establishment of an International Trade Organisation with periodic conferences in the interim.

Once these ldc drafts had been submitted a change in direction on the institutional issue was noticeable. Ldcs now felt that part of the conference's success depended on adequate mechanisms for implementation of decisions taken. By this time Group B realised that a decision to bring about new institutional arrangements seemed inevitable.

The basic differences between the above two groups may be very briefly summarised as follows: The ldcs wanted an International Trade Organisation with eventual universal membership; the West was silent on this, but had moved closer to the ldc request of one responsibility of the conference being the review of organisational arrangements. The ldcs wished the conference to be an organisation of the General Assembly under Article 22 of the Charter, while the West agreed to abandon the idea that it should be convened by ECOSOC and proposed instead that the new arrangements should fall under Article 13 and Chapters IX and X of the Charter. The West proposed that the conference should report to the General Assembly through ECOSOC, but the ldcs suggested the standing committee should report to the conference and General Assembly. The West wished the members of the standing committee to be nominated by the conference and confirmed by ECOSOC; the ldcs wished members to be elected by the conference. The West wanted the functions of the conference and standing committee to be broadened but the competence of the conference to promote international trade to be restricted, while the ldcs wanted the new institution to have overall responsibility on trade matters. The ldcs requested at least three Commissions be set up, the

West only one (on commodities) at first. The ldcs wanted the new machinery to be able to negotiate on trade issues, while the West wanted the new institutions to study the legal basis for trade relations between ldcs and dcs. The main dispute however was concerned with voting. Indeed this issue was one of the most controversial raised during the conference, and gave rise to much discussion about voting procedures in general. The ldcs argued for a two-thirds majority for matters of substance, and a simple majority on all procedural matters. The dcs on the other hand wanted, in addition to the two-thirds majority on issues of substance, a majority of the 12 main trading states.

Many efforts were made to reach agreement, but finally the ldcs forced through a vote on their draft which they won by 83 votes to 20 with 3 abstentions. The efforts to compromise however continued and eventually an agreement on a conciliation mechanism was reached. The final recommendation setting up UNCTAD was accepted unanimously on 15 June, the General Assembly accepted this resolution on 30 December 1964, and UNCTAD became a permanent organ of the UN.

Commodities
The Final Act of UNCTAD I sought to regulate and stabilise commodity markets, and to offset the trend of deteriorating terms of trade by raising the primary commodity prices to a remunerative level. In order to try to secure improved access for primary commodities, UNCTAD I recommended a standstill provision whereby no new tariff or non-tariff barriers be created against such exports; the removal of existing obstacles to ldc exports; the discouragement in dcs of domestic policies which stimulated the uneconomic production of those primary products which ldcs export; and the abolition of existing special preferential arrangements between some dcs and some ldcs as soon as international measures could be applied, provided that the ldcs concerned received at least equivalent advantages.

Manufactures
At UNCTAD I emphasis was laid on primary commodities, although it was widely recognised that a major change towards manufactures was advisable for ldcs. It was agreed in principle that ldcs should diversify and expand their exports of manufactures and semi-manufactures, and not be limited to the exporting of commodities. To facilitate this, increased access for ldc products should be a major

trading principle, e.g. by the introduction of preferences on manufactured and semi-manufactured products.

Aid

UNCTAD I adopted measures to increase the flow of financial resources to ldcs, and aimed to decrease the outflow of invisible payments from ldcs to dcs. The phrase 'trade not aid' was often heard at the conference. There was nevertheless a stress on financing, and on the flow of aid resources. The conference adopted a target of aid to ldcs of 1 per cent of the combined national incomes of the dcs. With regard to terms of financing it was argued that short periods of repayment, high interest rates and tied aid had led to serious debt servicing problems for many ldcs. Thus UNCTAD recommended measures to ease this, e.g. repayment to be spread over longer periods of time, interest rates to be low, and loans not to be tied.

COMMENT AND CONCLUSION

Although UNCTAD I was greeted sceptically by many in the West, as newspaper reports of the time confirm, it was regarded by the Third World as extremely important.

The Third World was determined to make it work. The conference was not unduly disturbed by purely political issues which if the will were lacking could easily have disrupted it; instead its procedures were laid squarely upon its agreed agenda.

A measure of UNCTAD's importance is that the development debate was radically altered by it. A new institutional framework for continuing this debate was created; a new system of group negotiation was evolved; a new system of voting through conciliation techniques was agreed upon; new bureaucrats with special skills emerged in the ldcs; the differences of approach between the dcs and the ldcs became evident, and contributed to the creation of new kinds of relationships between them.

Perhaps the most widely discussed and significant event to emerge from the conference was the consolidation of the Group of 77. These issues of underdevelopment and the debate about it are still with us to be worked out, but the terms of that debate were transformed by the conference. The Group of 77 regarded it as marking the beginning of a new era in the evolution of international cooperation in the field of trade and development.

Consideration is now given in the next chapter to a review of developments during succeeding conferences, UNCTAD II, III, IV, V, held in 1968, 1972, 1976 and 1979.

2 UNCTAD II, III, IV, V 1968-79

UNCTAD II NEW DELHI 1968

From the beginning UNCTAD II was seen by the ldcs as concerned with practical results; its theme was 'Action and Achievement'. At the third session of the UNCTAD Board in 1966 the consensus was that the conference should be selective in its search to achieve practical results, and should concentrate on ways and means of implementing the recommendations of UNCTAD I. Raul Prebisch, its Secretary-General, made a statement in which he stressed that a clear difference should exist between the nature and scope of the agenda of UNCTAD I and II — 'In 1964 there was as yet no machinery for dealing with matters of trade and development and therefore it was justified to cover the whole range of problems in relation to trade and development ... It is not a matter of selecting what is more or less important but of choosing those matters concerning which concrete action may be envisaged.'[1] He then outlined the concept of the 'points of crystallisation' according to which certain topics should be singled out for specific emphasis.

Preliminaries

The ldcs submitted a draft provisional agenda for the conference which contained the same items as those which the Secretariat had compiled, but the language used emphasised the need for action. For example, where the Secretariat draft read 'the reduction and elimination of tariff and non-tariff barriers' the ldc draft read 'programme for the elimination of tariff and non-tariff barriers'.[2]

The General Assembly at its 21st session decided that UNCTAD II should be held from 1 February to 25 March 1968 at New Delhi. It stressed that the conference should 'concentrate in particular on a limited number of fundamental and specific subjects with a view to achieving practical and concrete results by means of negotiation aimed at serving the greatest measure of agreement'. ECOSOC later echoed this approach when it stated that preparatory work for the conference should facilitate 'practical and concrete results of benefit to world trade and particularly to developing countries'.

Western apprehension of the ldc approach to UNCTAD II was reflected in its reaction to a statement by UN Secretary-General U Thant in which he expressed 'fervent hope' that the 'Kennedy Round' (of trade negotiations) would be followed by a 'New Delhi Round' which would begin to complete the work that remained unfinished. This was incorporated in a draft resolution on the conference and provoked a number of OECD countries to object to it on the grounds that it could be construed as giving the conference a character which it would not, in their opinion, have. The US representative, for example, suggested that to call it the 'New Delhi Round' was misleading since 'round' had developed a special meaning after years of trade negotiations in GATT and the USA did not mean to enter into specific trade commitments at New Delhi so would not support the use of the word. Thus the OECD countries voted against the paragraph containing the offending phrase, and abstained when the resolution was voted on.

The fifth session of the UNCTAD Board (August–September 1967) formed the concluding stage of intergovernmental preparations for the conference. The statement of its president formulated the aims of the conference which were 'to re-evaluate the economic situation and its implications for the implementation of the recommendations of the first ... conference; to achieve, through appropriate forms of negotiation, specific results that ensure real progress in international co-operation for development; to explore and investigate matters requiring more thorough study before agreement can be envisaged.'

The Algiers charter

The Group of 77, then consisting of some 88 countries, met at Algiers in October 1967 to prepare for UNCTAD II. The result of its meeting was a document called 'the Algiers Charter' which formulated a joint position for the Group of 77 to present at UNCTAD. The Charter was distributed as an official document of the General Assembly and UNCTAD.

The Group of 77 also decided at Algiers to send some of its senior members to visit the industrialised countries with the purpose of informing and persuading their governments of the conclusions reached at Algiers. The teams were then expected to produce a set of compromise proposals on which to base discussions at UNCTAD. But the attempt was a failure, no links were created in this way between Algiers and the conference, and the task of explaining and discussing the Charter with the industrialised countries thus fell wholly upon the conference.

The conference
One hundred and twenty one states met at UNCTAD II in New Delhi on 1 February 1968. Mr Dinesh Singh, the Indian Minister of Commerce, was elected President of the conference, and a Bureau consisting of the officers and chairmen of the five main sessional committees was set up. Five committees and three working groups were established for detailed examination of the substantive items of the agenda.

Group positions within the conference
As well as delegations of member countries the conference was attended by representatives of regional economic commissions, specialised agencies, GATT and 21 other intergovernmental organisations while representatives of 14 non-governmental organisations were also present. The conference divided into 98 subgroups, and at one point no less than 60 different meetings were taking place simultaneously.

The Group of 77   The Group met before UNCTAD opened after separate meetings had been held by the Latin American, the African and the Asian members.
   One of the main reasons for the difficulties encountered in UNCTAD II, according to many observers, was the caucus-like manner in which various groups tended to operate. All the negotiations both in plenary sessions and committees were preceded by behind-the-scenes meetings of ldcs in which the hardest line generally prevailed. Thus the Algiers Charter served as a 'floor' for ldc demands rather than a set of aspirations.
   At one point UNCTAD's Secretary-General was reported[3] to have appealed, in a closed meeting of the Group of 77, for ldcs to adopt a moderate approach on various issues before the conference; in his view that was the right way to achieve concrete results. He considered the most promising area for advance to be the proposed Generalised System of Preferences (GSP) scheme. This exposed some differences within the Group since India's interest focused on manufactures and semi-manufactures, whereas to Africa the trade in processed agri-

cultural products was far more important. In any event only a few
countries from the Group were at this time in a position to derive substantial advantage from the GSP — India, Pakistan, Mexico, Brazil
and Nigeria.
Another problem the GSP issue caused within the Group of 77 was
the question of existing preferences for ex-colonies. African and
Indian delegates at the Commonwealth Trade Ministers Meeting
agreed to accept in principle a proposal to replace the Commonwealth
Preference System by a general preference scheme for ldcs, but they
demanded guarantees to make up possible marginal losses if they lost
their special access to Commonwealth markets.

Group B   The Western developed countries   One Western newspaper report suggested that 'If the UNCTAD in New Delhi continues
as badly as it has begun, the outlook for the developing countries is
glum'.[4] USA and France resisted ldc pressure to overcome the trade
bias against them, while France, USA and West Germany were against
the straightforward increase in aid in the immediate future.
Events were made worse by the rush for gold in various European
capitals during the conference. At that time the general opinion
among Western delegates was that even if UNCTAD completed its
scheduled work, effective business was unlikely to be transacted while
the gold rush continued.
On the other hand the US sought to make a positive contribution to
UNCTAD II partly to compensate for its negative attitude at
UNCTAD I. Its Treasury was still lukewarm but the State Department
was keen to use the conference to improve the US image. However
owing to the difficulties of the dollar and powerful Congressional
lobbies the only real area for the US to develop was that of preferences. In 1967 President Johnson had pledged at Punta del Este,
Uruguay, to improve the access of ldcs to the US market, and he
informed the Latin Americans that Washington had come to accept
the principle of tariff preferences for manufactured products without
demanding matching preferences from them; but France was in
favour of reverse preferences. On this issue the ldcs hoped for support
from the more liberal developed countries like Italy, Holland, Den-
mark and Sweden.

Group D   The Eastern bloc countries   The Soviet Union took a
tougher opening stance than the West at UNCTAD, virtually ignoring
the few demands made upon the Communist camp by the ldcs. Mr N.

S. Patolichev, the Soviet Union Minister of Foreign Trade, told the conference that responsibility for development rested chiefly on the West. The USSR declared 'full support'[5] for the demands put forward by ldcs in the Algiers Charter, but suggested they look to capitalist countries for satisfaction.

However, later in the conference, while Group B was still hesitating to produce concrete proposals, the Eastern bloc announced specific measures designed to help ldc trade. The Bulgarian delegate submitted to the fifth committee a resolution on behalf of the socialist countries of Eastern Europe outlining a programme of action by them to promote ldc trade. He also appealed to ldcs to try to facilitate the implementation of these measures, and to accord to the socialist countries conditions for trade not less favourable than those granted to the other developed market economy countries.

Comment and conclusion

After eight weeks of deliberation the report of UNCTAD II was presented to the General Assembly on 29 March 1968.

The Secretary-General, Mr Prebisch, summarised the results of the conference under four broad points: (1) some limited and incomplete results with regard to fundamental problems of preference and finance; (2) some positive results in the spheres of trade expansion among ldcs, trade with socialist countries, shipping, the food problem, and policy in relation to least developed and land-locked countries; (3) virtually no results from ldc efforts to formulate measures on access to markets; (4) no contribution to the formulation of a global strategy for development.

He refused to attribute these unsatisfactory results to the short-comings of UNCTAD, but instead blamed a lack of political will. He argued that the group system of negotiation, although having potential, demonstrated certain shortcomings which were emphasised at the conference. In his view UNCTAD had not sufficiently facilitated the preparation of joint positions, nor encouraged inter-group communication.

The most successful outcome of UNCTAD II was the passing of a resolution on trade preferences, committing the rich countries for the first time to give special consideration in their import policies to all manufactured and semi-manufactured products from ldcs. However no deadline was set for the introduction of these preferences, and there were no concessions to the African states for preferences on processed agricultural products. Nor would the USA agree to the proposal until a timetable had been established for the abolition of reverse preferences by the French-speaking African states in favour of France, and some Commonwealth countries in favour of the UK.

In terms of aid an international target based on 1 per cent of the GNPs of the developed countries was agreed, but only some dcs accepted a date for the target. With regard to commodities the agreements reached held out hope of further marketing arrangements for more primary products than hitherto, but there remained many areas of disagreement in this field.

On balance UNCTAD II was not a success. The Brazilian delegate, making it clear that he spoke on behalf of the Group of 77, denounced the conference as 'far short of expectations of the ldcs' and amounting to 'no more than a few hesitant steps' in the right direction.[6] Some press reports were wholly pessimistic — the *Guardian* for example declared 'UNCTAD II seems to have been an almost total failure'. The Indian Chairman of UNCTAD II summed up the proceedings as containing 'many disappointments and some advances'.[7]

UNCTAD III SANTIAGO 1972

The Lima conference
In preparation for UNCTAD III the Group of 77 (some 95 nations) met at Lima in November 1971 in an attempt to work out a common Third World approach to present at Santiago.

The proceedings of three earlier ldc meetings had to be consolidated at Lima. These had resulted in the Bangkok Declaration of the Asians, the Addis Ababa Declaration of the Africans and the Lima Consensus of the Latin Americans. It proved to be no easy task, especially since it involved reconciling Latin American and African needs. At Lima the Latin Americans were radical, calling for a complete revision of the structure of UNCTAD and a world monetary conference to deal with the international monetary crisis. They were concerned with environmental and other questions like the impact of seabed mining on the economies of ldcs, which seemed irrelevant to the Africans, who were more worried about such matters as the lack of help for the least developed countries. Nor could they support the Latin American proposal to institutionalise the Group of 77 by setting up offices for it at Geneva.

One major gain for the Africans was the support they were able to get for their view that countries producing raw materials and basic commodities should present a united front in their dealings with the developed countries; most Latin Americans preferred to depend on their special arrangements with the USA for access to North American markets. Thus Lima emphasised the real differences in levels of development between the poor and poorest nations.

In November 1971 the conference produced the 'Declaration and Principles of the Action Programme of Lima', which was presented to the UN General Assembly. It reaffirmed the objectives of the Charter of Algiers, called on the USA to remove its 10 per cent surcharge on imports from ldcs and urged other developed countries to refrain from imposing similar restrictions. The declaration called on industrialised countries to establish the Generalised System of Preferences (GSPs) favouring ldcs, and appealed to the US to reconsider a senate decision halting its foreign aid programme. It recognised the authority of the International Monetary Fund (IMF) in dealing with financial problems, but asked for increased IMF voting rights for ldcs. Lima took place against the background of a monetary crisis precipitated by President Nixon's August measures. Thus it was preoccupied with reform of the international monetary system, and an intergovernmental Group of Twenty-four was set up to consider necessary action to counterbalance the Group of Ten. The conference reaffirmed the ldcs' faith in international cooperation for development, and expressed the belief that UNCTAD would provide a new opportunity to make a definitive collective effort to correct the unfavourable position in which the ldcs found themselves. The final document also urged developed countries to support certain basic principles in the sphere of international trade and development. After Lima the problems likely to arise at UNCTAD III were apparent.

The conference
On 13 April 1972 delegates from some 146 countries met in Santiago, Chile, for UNCTAD III. Raul Prebisch had resigned as Secretary-General in March 1969 with the following words 'If we do not succeed in effective and vigorous economic development the alternatives are clear. The deteriorating situation in the have-not countries will demonstrate that the extremists are right. Black power, now merely a US phenomenon, will become brown, yellow, and black power on a world scale.'[8]

Group positions within the conference

The Group of 77   The Third World's position may be summarised as

(i) The implementation of resolutions passed by UNCTAD I and II. These included the commitment by the developed countries to devote 1 per cent of their GNPs to world development; ldcs now wished to redefine the nature of this 1 per cent target. Also, in the four years since UNCTAD II, the USA had refused to implement the agreement by developed countries to grant duty-free access to its markets for the manufactured goods of the ldcs. (ii) The Group of 77 wanted the developed countries, particularly the USA, to accept that new issues of Special Drawing Rights (SDRs) would be channeled to ldcs as an automatic increment to aid flow. This was referred to as 'the link', and formed the main item of ldc demands. (iii) The Third World also required a guarantee to ldcs of the opportunity to supply an increasing share of developed country needs for commodities like sugar, rice, cotton, tobacco, meat and cereals.

As the Lima conference showed, many divisions existed within the Group of 77. An example of the problems this produced may be seen from the ldc approach to the question of the link. Two issues were under debate: how should the link actually work, and should the monetary system be overhauled to reduce the dominance of the more wealthy. The final ldc formulation was that SDRs should be used for additional development finance. However their debate took so long that they did not table their minimum resolution until the closing stages of the conference, and this meant that they were unable to take advantage of the developed countries' initial lack of hostility towards the link.

There was much ldc discontent expressed with the EEC's policy towards the Third World, and this was heightened by the UK's entry. A motion by 51 nations, including some of the Commonwealth countries and the entire Latin American bloc, sought 'concomitant obligations' in order to protect the trading patterns of the ldcs and to persuade the EEC to adopt more outward-looking policies. However the Group was very much divided on this issue.

Group B The countries of the developed West were preoccupied with their own problems at this time. It was US presidential election year, the European Common Market was about to be enlarged, and severe world monetary problems had reduced ldc purchasing power through the devaluation of the dollar so that the US aid programme was cut and the preference scheme delayed.

Nevertheless Dr Sicco Mansholt, the President of the European Commission, supported more favourable treatment of the ldcs, inviting UNCTAD to call on the dcs to open their markets so that a 15 per cent annual increase in exports of ldc manufactured goods would be possible, and suggesting that the industrialised nations be asked to allocate future issues of 'paper gold' within the IMF to take the special interests of the ldcs into account.

The essential points of the EEC position at UNCTAD III were outlined by Gaston Thorn, the Luxemburg Foreign Minister and then President of the Council of Ministers:[9] the least developed countries were to be given priority, and a specific aid programme was to be set up; attention was to be given to the purchasing power of ldcs and the EEC was ready to consider adjustments to the terms of trade and price structure for their basic products; the EEC was ready to consider improving and expanding the present system of GSPs; world monetary policy must take account of the special needs to ldcs, and in order to increase their exports it would not be enough simply to open up the markets of the developed countries; ldcs should be helped to build up economic integration among themselves on a regional basis.

Despite this the OECD countries at UNCTAD III were united in granting very few concessions to the ldcs. Indeed in the UK, as a result, government representatives were subjected to much criticism by the opposition spokesman on overseas development, Judith Hart, who called the British delegation 'entirely naive' or 'positively obstructive'. One comment made at the time was 'The patent unwillingness of the rich countries to make concessions to the poor countries on trade or aid, as evidenced in Santiago, should mark the awakening of the latter to the need for more active and aggressive policies.'[10]

Group D   The Eastern bloc appeared on the defensive against the Third World at UNCTAD. In his speech the Soviet Minister of Foreign Trade rejected the thesis, current among some members of the Group of 77, which referred to the socialist and Western countries together as 'the rich North'. He claimed that the Soviet five-year plan provided for further expansion of long-term credits at low interest rates to ldcs. In general however, at UNCTAD III the USSR seemed primarily concerned to further *détente* with the West and to pursue its quarrel with China.

Comment and conclusion

The conference was extremely disappointing for the Group of 77, and accomplished less than either UNCTAD I or II. Virtually its only achievement was an agreement for the developed countries to give special treatment to the poorest ldcs. On the central issue of monetary reform no substantial agreement was reached, although a compromise resolution was passed. This recognised that a more satisfactory system of monetary cooperation with the widest possible participation of developed and developing countries was desirable, and urged that since problems in the monetary, trade and financial areas should be resolved in a coordinated manner, UNCTAD's Secretary-General should consult the IMF and GATT.

The feelings of the Group of 77 after the conference are perhaps best described by Malaysia's chief delegate who said 'The stark reality is that the developed countries are not prepared to make any real concessions ... One has to be very naive to believe in future prospects.'[11] Indeed UNCTAD III served to reinforce a growing criticism of economic cooperation between the developed countries and the Third World, lending support to the Chinese thesis of self help expounded at the conference.

Despite its few achievements, the first real step towards the Third World's later demands for a New International Economic Order had been taken in the form of the 'Charter of Economic Rights and Duties of States' which was proposed at UNCTAD III.[12] This was completed by the General Assembly in 1974.

UNCTAD IV   NAIROBI 1976

UNCTAD IV took place at a time when Third World demands for a New International Economic Order had been launched, and the issue of underdevelopment and the relationship of ldcs with the developed countries was under wide discussion. A number of most important relevant events had taken place since UNCTAD III.[13] Of these the Sixth and Seventh Special Sessions of the United Nations (discussed in a later chapter) were of particular significance; the widespread feeling after the Seventh Special Session was that confrontation between rich and poor countries had been avoided, and that a cooperative course was now set in terms of 'North–South dialogue'.

In order to make UNCTAD IV less unwieldy than its predecessors it was agreed to reduce its agenda to nine major items, to keep the conference as short as possible (some three and a half weeks) and to reduce the amount of documentation. Another plan was to try to have a set of concrete and prenegotiated resolutions ready for discussion. These were to be thrashed out in Geneva during the meeting of the Trade and Development Board of UNCTAD, 8–19 March 1976. The outcome of the meeting was most disappointing. It aimed at broad agreement, for draft recommendations to submit to UNCTAD IV where this was the case and tentative solutions to be suggested where it was not. No agreement was reached at the meeting, not even for a 'conclusion' statement; even the use of the term 'New International Economic Order' was considered provocative by certain hardliners.

Third World countries met in Manila in August 1976 to prepare for UNCTAD IV. The Group of 77 later adhered as a group to their negotiating position, as it was outlined in the Manila Declaration (and Programme of Action)[14] to the end of the Nairobi meeting. However the accommodation given to certain areas of conflict within the Third World made some of the language of the Manila document extremely imprecise. It dealt with a number of complex requirements under each of the following topics — commodities, improvements to the IMF, manufactures and semi-manufactures, debt.

The conference
At UNCTAD IV the Third World warned that relations between developed and less developed countries would be 'poisoned' if Nairobi failed, and the 19 ldcs at the Conference on International Economic Cooperation (CIEC) in Paris warned that that too would be jeopardised unless 'substantial results' emerged from UNCTAD IV.

The agenda of UNCTAD IV contained nine substantive items to be discussed in five negotiating groups at Nairobi: Group I Commodities; Group II Manufactures, multilateral trade negotiations, transfer of technology; Group III Money and finance; Group IV Least developed, developing, island and landlocked countries, economic cooperation among developing countries; Group V Trade relations among countries having different economic and social systems, institutional issues.

Group positions within the conference

The Group of 77   The Group was now supported by the Organisation of Petroleum Exporting Countries (OPEC), which decided to freeze oil prices for the immediate future, and furthermore made it clear that if agreement was not reached on the plans of the ldcs to set up a £3 billion (UK) commodity fund, it was prepared to withdraw any cooperation with the West on oil. Some of the Group of 77 had hoped for more forceful backing from OPEC for the Manila Declaration, and on 10 May Manuel Perez-Guerero representing Venezuela, and a former UNCTAD Secretary-General, went to Paris to ask OPEC members for cash support for the Common Fund.[15] OPEC would not agree to this, although it did pledge £400 million to the International Fund for Agricultural Development, while some of its individual member countries like Kuwait and Saudi Arabia announced cash contributions to the fund.

The Group of 77 felt it could rely on the developed countries to continue negotiating, for several reasons. First, their desire for a successful CIEC. Secondly, divisions within their ranks. It was calculated that for political reasons the USA, West Germany and the other countries adopting a hard line at UNCTAD might feel they should compromise with the other 16 dcs which supported the Common Fund. Thirdly, in 1975 at Dakar the ldcs had met in the Conference of Developing Countries on Raw Materials. This resulted in an agreement to set up producers' associations grouped in a council for consultation and cooperation, and backed by a fund, known as the Dakar Fund. This was seen as demonstrating ldc capacity and intent (if necessary) for self-reliance.

The unity of the Group of 77 was strong at UNCTAD IV, and based on the Manila Declaration. However, there was naturally some dissension. India, Malaysia and Kenya were more moderate in their demands than most other ldcs while the Africans tended to disagree with the rest of the group on some issues.

Group B The Western developed countries, in contrast to the Group of 77, were very much divided. They could no longer present a stone wall to the Third World as they had at UNCTAD III; total resistance was no longer seen as a feasible policy. Unlike the Group of 77, Group B had not agreed on a common policy before UNCTAD IV. The main cause of division was their varying policies towards the proposed Common Fund. The dispute was concerned with how far the EEC should be committed to setting up the Common Fund which was regarded by the ldcs as essential for the New International Economic Order; the disputed paragraph provided for an early examination of 'a possible coordinating financing facility, or Common Fund', and aimed at starting negotiations to set it up within two years. This was strongly opposed by the UK, West Germany, Japan and the USA but accepted by 17 other developed countries. The opposite poles were represented by the Netherlands which wanted a firm commitment to the Common Fund, and by West Germany which refused to accept even any explicit mention of it. The Dutch Development Cooperation Minister, Jan Pronk, played a prominent part in preventing a final clash.

With the failure of the dcs to agree on a common negotiating position after two days, the Group of 77 submitted their own draft resolution. Based largely on the Manila proposals it encouraged the more sympathetic developed countries to break from the rest. Eventually, the small group of ministers at UNCTAD took over the task of reaching a compromise based on the text put forward by the Group of 77. This dealt with four main points — objectives, commodity coverage, international measures and procedures, timetable.

Group D   The conference was marked by a Sino-Soviet clash in which the Chinese Deputy Minister of Foreign Trade, Zhou Huamin, launched an attack on the Soviet Union. 'This Superpower' he said 'is even more greedy and more cruel than old time imperialism in its plunder and exploitation of the Third World.' The Soviet Foreign Trade Minister later commented that this was designed to undermine the solidarity of the forces fighting to 'liquidate the old economic order'.

The Third World continued its criticism of the socialist countries for their lack of readiness to meet its needs, as exemplified by Group D's rejection of the ldcs' main demands of commitment to an aid target of 1 per cent of GNP, and the payment in hard currency for ldc exports.

Comment and conclusion
UNCTAD IV ended just before dawn on 31 May with two main achievements:

1. A last minute compromise on the Common Fund. This provided for preparatory studies to be followed by a full-scale negotiating conference to be held not later than the following March. However it was made clear by the UK, USA, and West Germany that this did not imply a commitment on their part to the Fund, and indeed there was no stipulation that these negotiations would have a terminal date.

2. A resolution on debt simply welcomed a pledge by the developed countries to respond in a multilateral framework to individual requests for rescheduling, but a much stronger resolution proposed by the Group of 77 recommending a major debt conference under UNCTAD was also adopted. The USSR emphasised that these resolu-

tions could not apply to Eastern Europe because credit arrangements with ldcs there were on a different basis.

The dcs also supported resolutions to increase the transfer of technology to ldcs, but insisted that all such exchanges must accord with contractual obligations and must respect the confidentiality of technical information.

The Third World expected a great deal from UNCTAD IV. It had followed upon the Seventh Special Session, it came after the Lomé Convention had been signed with the EEC, and Commonwealth countries expected some further progress after Kingston and Georgetown. Because of the divisions within the developed countries it was difficult to proceed towards serious future negotiations; and the UK in particular disappointed the Commonwealth countries. Even a 'Nairobi Declaration', hoped for by President Kenyatta of Kenya, proved impossible.

Nevertheless a formal conclusion to the conference was reached without open conflict. One Third World delegate said that UNCTAD IV had produced only a first round victory in its attempt to force the USA and its allies to accept the Common Fund, but Herbert Walker of Jamaica, a spokesman of the Group of 77, described the Common Fund resolution as a turning point in international economic relations. Although it was only a 'poor shadow' of what was really needed, it resulted from genuine attempts to accommodate different views. Another delegate claimed 'We have won a moral victory here', and indeed most ldcs seemed to feel that enough progress had been made for the North–South conference to resume in Paris in a reasonably favourable political climate. The EEC Commissioner for Development felt that the importance of UNCTAD IV was that it allowed many problems to be clearly defined — its tangible results were few, but it was a starting point for continuing mandatory negotiations.

Further negotiations were agreed to at UNCTAD IV as a follow-up to the conference, for example a negotiating conference on the Common Fund was to be held by March 1979, as well as preparatory meetings on individual commodity arrangements leading to formal negotiations.

UNCTAD V   MANILA 1979

UNCTAD V and 1979 arrived, but the New International Economic Order patently had not. The issues discussed at Manila were very much the same as those considered at UNCTAD IV at Nairobi in 1976 but instead of launching new initiatives in the North–South debate, the conference was more concerned with consolidating the very limited advantages made since UNCTAD IV. Its mood was generally sceptical and depressed mainly because of the worsening economic situation in the developed world which was seen to be affecting all areas of North–South negotiations, e.g. the Conference on International Economic Cooperation. 1980 marks the start of the Third United Nations Development Decade, and UNCTAD V had to some extent to lay the framework for this. More important however was the need to make some progress in altering the balance and structure which governs international economic relationships; this was the political goal, and the method followed at Manila was to consolidate advances already made.

Progress since 1976

Commodities
UNCTAD IV had concentrated upon the demand for a Common Fund for stabilising the prices of 18 commodities within an integrated programme. In March 1979 agreement was reached on setting up the Fund at the fourth UNCTAD conference on a Common Fund. The imminence of UNCTAD V gave impetus to the negotiations which since 1976 had been constant although usually deadlocked. It now seems that the Fund could come into operation by 1981. It is to have two 'windows'. The first, with initial capital of $400 million, is to link buffer stocking commodity agreements; stocks of ten key commodities will be bought and sold to regulate prices. The second 'window' is to finance measures in commodities which cannot be stocked. It will have $70 million in guaranteed initial finance, and a further $280 million is hoped for through voluntary contributions. But the Fund is much reduced from Third World original financial expectations.

Protectionism
This issue emerged as central in UNCTAD V. The Multilateral Trade Negotiations (the 'Tokyo Round') held under the auspices of GATT in Geneva, were galvanised by the prospect of UNCTAD V into an agreement on 11 April, after over five years of discussions. Third World delegations reluctantly agreed to the principle of selective safeguards against imports, provided a code was formulated to limit their functioning. This was demanded by the EEC in order to protect

the European market against disruption by cheap imports. Further details were to be worked out at Manila. With regard to the issue of subsidies and countervailing duties, Third World negotiators accepted limitations on their use of export subsidies. This was agreed provided the USA submits to an 'injury test' before applying countervailing duties on subsidised imports. The Multilateral Trade Negotiation agreement has not opened up developed country markets to the Third World, but simply cut tariff schedules by an average of 28–32 per cent over the next five to eight years.[16] These negotiations were really a holding operation, and not a step towards restructuring developed country industries.

Debts and loans

Since Nairobi eleven donor countries of the OECD have provided debt relief amounting to $6.5 billion (UK). Aid donors agreed at an UNCTAD meeting in March 1978 to cancel or convert to grants the official development assistance debts[17] of the least developed countries. With regard to loans, the IMF has developed its lending capacity to some ldcs since 1976.[18] Its regular Special Drawing Rights allocations were increased in October 1978 by 50 per cent; the supplementary financing facility began in February 1979 to help members who need larger and longer-term loans; the Trust Fund now lends to low-income ldcs at a concessional interest rate for as long as ten years; the liberalised compensatory financing facility provides compensation for shortfalls in export earnings from any single commodity.

Preliminaries

The Arusha Charter

The Group of 77, Group A and Group C of UNCTAD, met at Arusha in Tanzania from 6–16 February 1979. A joint strategy was agreed on, outlined in the Arusha Charter,[19] as a framework for negotiations at UNCTAD. 'Deep disappointment' was expressed about the slow progress made since UNCTAD IV towards a New International Economic Order.

The following main points were outlined in the Charter, and set the terms of the debate at UNCTAD V:

Trade The Charter called on the developed countries to restructure their industries in such a way as to permit ldcs a 25 per cent share in the world production of manufactures, and a 35 per cent share in its trade; to achieve this a more democratic decision-making structure was called for. Protectionism was condemned, and the recent conclusions of GATT's Multilateral Trade Negotiations criticised; a special body, it was argued, should be set up in UNCTAD to guard against protectionist trends. Another body should also be set up to review and recommend progress towards the New International Economic Order (NIEO). The Generalised System of Preferences favouring ldcs should be made permanent.

Commodities   Voluntary contributions to the second 'window' of the Common Fund were sought. 'Development aspects' (like local processing) of commodity production should be given priority. Negotiations on commodities should be speeded up. There should be a new complementary financing facility in the IMF to compensate Third World commodity producers for loss of earnings.

Finance   A new international commission on debt should be set up. Aid levels should be raised. There should be 'a genuine and fundamental reform of the International Monetary system' and an 'equitable decision-making process in the Bretton Woods institutions'[20]

Shipping and technology   A cargo-sharing deal for bulk carriers was sought, as well as ways of phasing out 'flags of convenience' fleets. With regard to technology the Arusha Charter asked for a binding internationally agreed code of conduct.

Economic cooperation between developing countries   Arusha sought measures for UNCTAD to promote this, e.g. through regional meetings of ldcs.

Group B
The developed countries made less obvious preparations for UNCTAD V, although its issues certainly were discussed and positions agreed on beforehand. Their main preoccupations however were with their domestic affairs and the problems of economic recession, as was made clear at the European summit in early March 1979. The EEC regarded its main contribution to the North–South dialogue to be the renegotiation of the Lomé Agreement which regulated its trade with 57 African, Caribbean and Pacific nations.

The conference
UNCTAD V began in Manila on 7 May 1979. President Marcos of the Philippines opened the conference and urged the delegates from 154 countries to work towards a new international economic order. Señor Carlos Romero was elected conference president.

The problem of growing protectionism in the developed countries emerged in the first week, ldc discontent having been further aroused by the GATT Multilateral Trade Negotiations which empowered the dcs to use safeguard clauses against imports. The EEC defended its record on trade liberalisation, the Economics Minister of France warned that the pessimism of many ldcs on the trade question entailed great risks in underestimating attempts to treat ldcs positively, the Australian Prime Minister joined the Third World in accusing the EEC of adopting protectionist trade policies.[21]

The start of serious negotiations at UNCTAD was delayed, mainly because of problems of establishing unity which emerged within the ldcs. These developed because of ldc oil importers' quarrels with the oil exporting countries which they argued were not sufficiently compensating the ldcs for oil price rises. Costa Rica proposed that energy should be discussed as a most important issue. The developed countries supported this, along with Colombia, Central America, Argentina and Chile, but other ldcs insisted that UNCTAD was not the best forum for this issue; they felt the ldcs should concentrate on finance, trade and technology. Many African countries took this line, anxious not to jeopardise OPEC's offer to contribute the poorest countries' share to the Common Fund for commodities. Iraq attempted to counter such criticism by proposing a new international fund to compensate the ldcs for price increases while Venezuela attempted to mediate between the two groups. This discussion marked the point at which the ldcs' ambiguous attitude towards OPEC came into the open. On the one hand OPEC was regarded by them as the model for Third World commodity organisation and power against the developed world, but on the other hand ldcs suffered badly from the increased oil prices and from the growing inflation in the West. It was finally agreed that energy should not be part of ongoing negotiations at the conference, although the developed countries refused to withdraw it from the UNCTAD V agenda. Further consideration of OPEC is deferred to a later chapter.

Other disputes also disrupted the conference. Some 30 Arab delegates and their supporters walked out over the Arab–Israeli conflict, and 13 Soviet Union-allied countries walked out during an address made by the deposed Cambodian rulers. Another deadlock developed, towards the end of the conference, over proposals to reform the world monetary system. The IMF in particular was criticised by the Third World, and this dispute over an issue at the heart of ldc demands for a reformed economic order led to threats of withdrawal by both the African group and the USA.

Comment and conclusion
UNCTAD V was generally regarded as a failure. Headlines such as 'A Tale of Disappointments'[22] and 'Failure at Manila'[23] summed up the final meetings. No agreement was reached, even on a compromise declaration. One of UNCTAD's main failures was its inability to achieve any agreement on developing itself institutionally; the Group of 77's aim to strengthen UNCTAD as the sole forum for North–South negotiations was rejected by the developed countries, and this meant that GATT and the IMF (and thus the much-criticised old power base) once again had to be relied on.

The main results of the conference were as follows:[24]

(a) A Programme of Action for the least developed countries was agreed upon, including a request for 'much larger flows' of assistance to those countries; but no promises were secured.

(b) Thirteen countries pledged a total of $87 million to the second 'window' of the Common Fund for Commodities.

(c) Action on an international strategy to improve the technological capacity of the Third World was agreed to, but the main issues blocking a code of conduct for the transfer of technology were not resolved.

(d) There was not resolution on the world trade and economic situation, nor on any structural changes in the world economic order.

(e) Maritime countries committed themselves to ratify the 1974 Code of Conduct for the Shipowners' Association (known as 'liner conferences') but there was no agreement on other ldc shipping demands.

(f) UNCTAD's support activities for economic cooperation among ldcs, it was agreed, should be intensified; and UNCTAD was to help in convening a special session of the committee in the 1980s.

The failure of UNCTAD V raises a number of fundamental questions. Can much be expected from negotiations at a time of economic difficulty among the developed countries? Is a structural transformation of the world economic system possible through piecemeal negotiations at conferences such as UNCTAD? Or is a broad composite combination of different approaches called for by the Third World in its struggle against inbuilt poverty; and if so will this not lead to increased radicalism?

The Third World was in disarray at Manila, and its internal disputes for the first time disrupted an UNCTAD conference. It failed to make any impact upon the increasing protectionism of the developed countries, as indeed it did in its efforts to move forward to its major goal, a new international economic order.

After review of the UNCTAD conferences, following chapters are concerned with other organisations; they are interrelated both with UNCTAD and with each other in their relevance to the organisation of the Third World.

3 The Non-aligned Movement

The debate about what non-alignment means began in the 1950s and continues today, during and after Havana. Its terms have changed, but the questions still reflect doubts about its meaning, and indeed relevance. Definition is difficult. But the countries concerned continue to meet; and in so doing they reflect the moods and events of the Third World whose perception of itself and its problems is of the utmost importance in understanding the development of the movement. Perhaps non-alignment can best be understood as 'an aspiration towards a general coexistence of nations and states regardless of their size, economic power, differences in social and political systems, in race, religion, language or historical and cultural heritage. Non-alignment is a long-term policy, something more than the mere holding of occasional meetings which, regardless of the number of participants and level, have the exclusive character of consultations before a new action.'[1]

The non-aligned movement is considered in this chapter, largely through review of its meetings. Its member nations are listed in Table 3.1.

The post-war world presented a new and different framework for action by the poor countries. Wartime experiences and the beginnings of independence for colonies had widened perspectives. The United Nations provided a forum for continuity of expression and collective action, although the general attitude of ldcs towards it was ambiguous. They were torn between the possibility of using it as an instrument towards their political ends or of superseding it with their own autonomous organisations, as India's Prime Minister, Mr Nehru suggested. Afro-Asian states first tried to gain multilateral contacts and greater cohesion, but with few positive results, through the medium of such international gatherings as: the Asian Relations Con-

TABLE 3.1
Non-aligned movement member states 1979

Afghanistan	Iran	Rwanda
Algeria	Iraq	Sao Tome and
Angola	Ivory Coast	Principe
Argentina	Jamaica	Saudi Arabia
Bahrain	Jordan	Seychelles
Bangladesh	Kampuchea	Senegal
Belize	Kenya	Sierra Leone
Benin	Korea (Democratic	Singapore
Bhutan	Peoples' Republic	Somalia
Bolivia	of)	South West African
Botswana	Kuwait	People's
Burundi	Laos	Organisation
Cameroon (United	Lebanon	(SWAPO)
Republic of)	Lesotho	Sri Lanka
Cape Verde	Liberia	Sudan
Central African	Libyan Arab Republic	Surinam
Republic	Madagascar	Swaziland
Chad	Malawi	Syrian Arab Republic
Comoros	Malaysia	Tanzania
Congo	Maldives	Togo
Cuba	Mali	Trinidad and Tobago
Cyprus	Malta	Tunisia
Djibouti	Mauritania	Uganda
Dominica	Mauritius	United Arab Emirates
Egypt (Arab Republic	Morocco	Upper Volta
of)	Mozambique	Vietnam (Socialist
Equatorial Guinea	Nepal	Republic of)
Ethiopia	Nicaragua	Yemen Arab Republic
Gabon	Niger	Yemen's People's
Gambia	Nigeria	Democratic
Ghana	Oman	Republic
Grenada	Pakistan	Yugoslavia
Guinea	Palestine Liberation	Zaire
Guinea-Bissau	Organisation (PLO)	Zambia
Guyana	Panama	Zimbabwean Patriotic
India	Peru	Front
Indonesia	Qatar	

Burma resigned in late 1979

ference of 1947 at New Delhi; the New Delhi Meeting of 1949 at which the Indonesian question was considered and from which the 'Colombo Group' of 1954 emerged; the abortive Baguio Conference held in the Philippines in May 1950 to consider regional questions; and the Asian Socialist International which was set up in January 1953.

Afro-Asian dissatisfaction with the UN was first expressed when their vote in the General Assembly became more important after the 'Uniting for Peace' resolution of November 1950. In October 1951 Egypt's Foreign Minister requested the Secretary-General to place on the agenda a complaint regarding the situation in Morocco. Some months later 11 Afro-Asian states sought to bring the Tunisian situation to the Council's attention. This request was turned down, but it led them to the formation of the Afro-Asian Group, or the 'Group of Thirteen'; the countries concerned were Afghanistan, Burma, Egypt, India, Indonesia, Iraq, Lebanon, Pakistan, Persia, Philippines, Saudi Arabia, Syria, Yemen, and sometimes Ethiopia, Liberia and some Latin America states.

The first sustained effort to organise outside the UN took place in 1954. A meeting of statesmen from India, Burma, Ceylon, Pakistan and Indonesia took place at Colombo in May, in order to consider possible action in connection with the situation in Indo-China. However the states concerned then constituted themselves as sponsors of an intended Afro-Asian conference, and these 'Colombo Powers' came to represent a potential nucleus for an Afro-Asian international organisation. The Bogor conference in December 1954 was held near Jakarta to continue these arrangements and it was agreed that the first objective must be to draw in as many Afro-Asian states as possible, irrespective of political differences. A brief non-controversial agenda was prepared for Bandung.

THE BANDUNG ASIAN–AFRICAN CONFERENCE   INDONESIA 1955

Bandung was important more as a symbol of a new dimension in world affairs than for its results. It represented for the first time in the post-war world and on this scale, the confluence of the emerging forces of Asia and Africa. The core of its philosophy was represented in the famous 'Panshilah', or Five Principles, first formulated by China and India in 1954. These may be summarised as: mutual respect for each others' territory; non-interference in other countries' internal affairs; equality and mutual benefit; peaceful co-existence; and non-aggression.[2]

The participants

Bandung was essentially a meeting of Asian and Middle Eastern countries, although a few from central Africa attended — the Gold Coast, Liberia and the Sudan. At the time many of the non-aligned felt that both Communist China and the Soviet Union were closer to them in outlook than the Western countries who still controlled many African lands; this view was reflected in an invitation to China, and in the fact that there was a lively discussion before it was decided not to invite the Soviet Union.

According to press reports of the day many Western countries such as the UK, Australia and New Zealand were perturbed at not being invited, while the USA's main concern seemed to have been with the Chinese participation.

China in fact proved to be an important force at Bandung. Prime Minister Zhou Enlai seemed to create a good impression of peaceful intent on most countries present. Towards the end of the conference he raised the question of Formosa, but no motion regarding Chinese international status was included in the final communiqué.

One feature of Bandung was the fluidity of relationships among its 24 countries; those which agreed on certain issues differed on others. Debate on Communist subversion, agression and colonialism created the most definite alignments.

Results

Neither China nor the Soviet Union achieved any major victories at Bandung and many Western newspapers expressed relief after the conference, reporting that although Western colonialism had been well dragged through the dust, the dangers of Communism had also been convincingly brought out by many delegates.

In the final communiqué[3] there were pro-Western clauses encouraging economic cooperation with the West, and justifying membership of Asian–African nations in alliances like SEATO and NATO, while evidence of the anti-Communist majority was clear in that Communist China was not proposed for a United Nations seat. The pro-Western line was encouraged by the new US foreign aid programme which was launched during the time of the conference; it proposed aid of $3 billion (UK), with $1 billion of this to Asia.

Unanimous agreement was obtained on economic and cultural cooperation issues. It was recorded that 'This Afro-Asian conference marks a further epoch in the resurgence of Asia and Africa and in the determination of their peoples to take their rightful place in the comity of nations, and play their full part in the background of their national independence, safe-guarding their territories from intervention and infringement of exploitation by others, and thus to make their own contribution to world peace and the well-being of humanity as a whole.' This affirmation was confirmed in the Ten Principles of Coexistence:[3] Respect for fundamental human rights and for the purposes and principles of the Charter of the United Nations; respect for the sovereignty and territorial integrity of all nations; recognition of the equality of all races and of the equality of all nations large and small; abstention from intervention or interference in the international affairs of another country; respect for the right of each nation to defend itself singly or collectively, in conformity with the Charter of the United Nations; abstention from the use of arrangements of collective defence to serve the particular interests of any of the big powers, and abstention by any country from exerting pressure on other countries; refraining from acts or threats of aggression or the use of force against the territorial integrity or political independence of any country; settlement of all international disputes by peaceful means, such as negotiation, conciliation, arbitration or judicial settlement, as well as other peaceful means of the parties' own choice in conformity with the Charter of the United Nations; promotion of mutual interests and cooperation; respect for justice and international obligations.

BELGRADE 1961   FIRST SUMMIT CONFERENCE OF NON-ALIGNED COUNTRIES (Theme: world tension)

In 1959 President Tito conceived the need for a non-aligned meeting, when the Soviet Union and the Chinese launched their campaign to discredit Yugoslavia in Asia. However India's Prime Minister, Mr Nehru, was reluctant to sponsor a movement which could be regarded as resembling a new bloc between East and West, and this led to considerable discussion about the distinction between a 'bloc of non-aligned states' and a 'third force'. Finally after two years of pressure by Presidents Tito and Nasser on the one hand, and Sukarno on the other, India joined an uncommitted triumvirate in sponsoring the conference. Communist China did not want the non-aligned summit and sought to promote a second Asian–African conference like Bandung, where it had played an important role. Thus it supported Sukarno's initiative in March 1961 when he tried to persuade other governments to agree to a second Afro-Asian conference, suggesting that some countries which were not non-aligned but simply hostile to colonialism and imperialism should be invited.

The conference
The Belgrade conference took place against a background of a deteriorating international situation as a result of the Cold War and the crisis in Berlin, the turmoil in the Congo and the liberation struggle particularly in Algeria. The final report of its preparatory meeting held at Cairo in June 1961 declared: 'The Heads of States and Governments of 21 non-aligned countries suggested that in view of recent world developments and a dangerous increase of international tension a conference might be held towards improvement of international relations and the relinquishment of the policy of force and the constructive settlement of pending world issues and conflicts.'[4] This became the central theme at Belgrade. There India succeeded in emphasising the need for world peace rather than the more popular theme of anti-colonialism, despite considerable dissention, notably by the 'Casablanca' group led by Egypt, Ghana, Guinea, and their main allies which sought to form a distinct pressure group.

Results
In a statement on the dangers of war and the preservation of peace, the conference issued an appeal to the US and the Soviet Union to suspend their 'war preparations' and to make contact with each other in order to avert imminent conflict. A 27-point Declaration[5] was issued which also placed emphasis on the need to end colonialism, and upon other matters including the following: (a) In terms of President Tito's proposal for a world disarmament conference it argued that non-aligned nations should be represented at all future conferences on disarmament, and that general and complete disarmament should be guaranteed by an effective system of inspection and control. (b) A moratorium on the testing of all nuclear weapons was called for. The Soviet Union announcement that it intended to resume nuclear tests was greeted with dismay by the non-aligned who regarded this as a show of strength and a demonstration of disregard for non-aligned opinion. (c) The view of inevitable Cold War was rejected and the principles of peaceful coexistence were espoused. (d) Changes in the United Nations were sought. For example it was felt that membership of the Security Council and ECOSOC should be expanded, and that the secretariat be structured differently. But there was no support for

the Soviet Union view that the United Nations was an instrument of the West. (e) It was agreed that force should not be used to solve the German problem.

Non-alignment was given shape at the Belgrade summit, and all future non-aligned conferences followed from this. Non-alignment came to mean more than the Afro-Asianism of Bandung, and a policy of non-involvement as a formula for the preservation of international peace and security. It had now emerged as a synthesis termed non-alignment, an alternative to the division of the world into those Eastern and Western blocs which seemed unable to solve international issues.

CAIRO 1964   SECOND SUMMIT CONFERENCE (Theme: economic development)

Although the Soviet Union and China had become increasingly hostile towards one another the Cario conference faced no immediate world crisis as Belgrade had done, so the way was open for a move away from East–West differences towards a concentration on those between rich and poor countries. The Test Ban Treaty had been signed by the great powers, and the arms race had slowed down. The blocs too, so firmly established in 1961, were loosening; de Gaulle was asserting an independent role for France and Europe, while the Communists of eastern Europe, particularly Rumania, were pursuing policies more independent of the Soviet Union.

The prime forces behind Cairo were President Tito and Mr Nehru, who were anxious to hold a non-aligned conference similar to that of Belgrade before China could organise support for another possible Afro-Asian conference along the lines of Bandung. Both had reason to want to exclude China, which considered Tito's régime revisionist and was involved in a border flare-up with India. Mr Nehru was also anxious to exclude Pakistan from the conference, and this could be done if the membership criteria were the same as at Belgrade, thus excluding members of SEATO and CENTO.

The conference
Egypt's President Nasser presented the theme of the conference in his opening address. He argued that non-alignment would continue as long as peace based on justice had not been established in the world, and called for the gap between rich and poor to be narrowed. His

phrase 'poverty and wealth cannot peacefully coexist' helped to rein-
terpret the meaning of non-alignment in a changed international en-
vironment. Mrs Bandaranaike, Ceylon's Prime Minister, argued that
the triumph of non-alignment would lie in the ultimate elimination of
the need for its practice, and pursued its reinterpretation in the
following way. It had been remarked, she claimed, that since the 1961
Belgrade conference the improvement that had taken place in relations
between USA and the Soviet Union, together with other developments, necessitated a re-examination of the policy of non-alignment.
'We agree that no such policy can remain in a static condition,' she
said. Like all policies, non-alignment too had to be responsive to
changing circumstances, but the non-aligned must be careful that in
the process the concept of non-alignment did not lose its essence or its
identity. One way in which this could be achieved would be to trans-
late its objectives as much as possible into 'more precise measures of
policy'. The practical definition of non-alignment accepted for the
conference was the same as that used in Belgrade: no country with
foreign bases or military alliances with members of the great power
blocs could attend.

The issues of colonialism and racialism were bound to be strongly
felt and voiced at this conference, since more and more black African
countries had joined the non-aligned movement. Nehru regarded these
issues as somewhat obsolete, and was more concerned with international questions; but India's vulnerable position with regard to
Pakistan and China meant that he had to pay some attention to them
in order to win support from the newly independent states. Prime
Minister Shastri, who attended after Mr Nehru's death, followed the
same policy.

There were representatives of 48 states as well as 11 observers
present at Cairo, making the conference twice as large as that held in
Belgrade. The reasons for this were the emergence of new independent
African states and the efforts of Nasser, Tito and Nehru to include
more European and Latin American nations. Tito was particularly
keen to interest European neutrals in order to balance the Afro-Asian
sympathy for the Chinese. Thus Sweden, Switzerland and Austria
were invited, but declined, and Finland sent an observer; from Latin
America only Cuba took full part in the conference, but other states
such as Mexico, Brazil, Chile, Venezuela, Uruguay, Ecuador and
Bolivia sent observers.

The conference began with great potential for discord, largely as a
result of the arguments between those endorsing and those rejecting

the 'Peking line' of confrontation with the West. President Sukarno with considerable support, was opposed to peaceful coexistence with the West, and in favour of the Chinese revolutionary struggle; Presidents Nasser and Tito, together with Prime Ministers Shastri and Bandaranaike, took the opposite view. The latter were optimistic, considering the world situation to have improved since the Belgrade conference, both in terms of world peace and help for the ldcs. Sukarno on the other hand was a pessimist, and considered the improved US and Soviet Union relations not to have helped the ldcs at all. He seemed to many at Cairo to extend his dispute with Malaysia into the realm of conflict between non-alignment and imperialism, calling it a 'new area of confrontation'. Like the Chinese he regarded peaceful co-existence as in opposition to the liberation struggle. Tito, Nasser and Shastri sought to show that the two were complementary and not antagonistic; to quote President Tito: 'It is obvious that there can be no peace without freedom but under the present conditions it's also true that there can be no freedom without peace.'[6] Ultimately the conference rejected the attempt to move away from the West and closer to China. But this was the first time that the question of confrontation with the West had been so closely argued among the non-aligned.

The ldcs at the conference also expressed apprehension that 'regional economic groupings of industrialised countries will adversely affect the interests of their economies if conceived and operated in a restrictive and discriminating manner'. This was taken to be an allusion to the European Economic Community, and caused some concern in the West that the Soviet Union intended to use the EEC to promote anti-Western feeling in the Third World.

Results

The Programme for Peace and International Cooperation[7] which was adopted at the end of the conference, had no dominant focus as at Belgrade in 1961 when an appeal was made to the USA and the Soviet Union to suspend their war preparations. It was presented under the following main headings:

1. Concerted action for the liberation of the countries still dependent; elimination of colonialism, neo-colonialism and imperialism. The areas under discussion were the Congo, Portugal and Southern Rhodesia.
2. Respect for the right of peoples to self-determination, and condem-

nation of the use of force against the exercise of this right.
3. Racial discrimination and the policy of apartheid.
4. Peaceful coexistence and the codification of its principles by the United Nations.
5. Respect for the sovereignty of states and their territorial integrity; problems of divided nations.
6. Settlement of disputes without threat or use of force in accordance with the principles of the UN Charter.
7. General and complete disarmament.
8. Military pacts, foreign troops and bases.
9. The United Nations' role in international affairs; implementation of its resolutions and amendment of its Charter.
10. Economic development and cooperation. This included support for the Declaration of the Group of 77, and an appeal for states to implement the Final Act of UNCTAD I. The conference also recommended that the target of economic growth set for the development decade by the United Nations should be revised upwards.
11. Cultural, scientific and educational cooperation, and consolidation of international and regional organisations working for this purpose.

LUSAKA 1970   THIRD SUMMIT CONFERENCE (Theme: economic self-reliance)

President Tito of Yugoslavia was again the prime mover in the convening of this summit, and mooted the idea in 1967. But this time India was reluctant to become involved. This change of attitude was widely discussed in the Indian press, which was often critical of non-alignment;[8] an article in the *Hindu* was headed 'The Twilight of Non-alignment',[9] and argued that the movement should more appropriately be called 'a conference of newly-independent states'; it noted that many African states were closely aligned with France, and others with the UK and South Africa. Eventually India's support for the conference was secured by Yugoslavia abandoning its attempt to open the ranks of the non-aligned to some states which were members of international defence pacts; its Foreign Minister announced 'the criteria of non-alignment defined in 1961 for the Belgrade summit and reaffirmed in the second conference in Cairo in 1964 are still valid'. India was thus reassured that Pakistan could not be considered for membership, and lent her support to the conference.

Tito's aim was that the conference be convened just before the 31st United Nations General Assembly in the autumn of 1970, so that a common non-aligned strategy could be agreed. He hoped to see non-alignment revitalised as a movement once more influential in world affairs. Since the mid 1960s the countries concerned had been preoccupied with their own problems, but now he suggested such a conference was vital for the strengthening of the United Nations.

Two views of non-alignment emerged at this stage. The first, propounded by Tito, who needed support for his stand against the Soviet Union, was that non-alignment should be a third force united by a desire for peaceful coexistence, and influential by virtue of its independence of existing power blocs. The second, put forward by the newly-emerging African states like Algeria and Zambia together with Cuba, supported a non-alignment which actively sought to influence world opinion, particularly against colonialism and imperialism.

The Organisation of African Unity had been formed at Addis Ababa, and now proved to be very influential at the third non-aligned summit. Lusaka was aptly chosen as its venue and Zambia's position along the frontier of white-ruled Southern Africa ensured that much of the conference would be focused on colonialism, racism and the liberation struggle in that area. President Kaunda encouraged support for the conference, and Finland, Mexico, Bolivia, Venezuela, Uruguay and Peru were invited to send observers, together with various liberation movements; 74 Heads of State were invited.

The conference theme

President Nyerere of Tanzania, in a major re-statement of non-alignment's role and meaning[10] provided the theme for the summit: economic self-reliance. Non-alignment was never a matter of neutrality or of treading a tightrope between contending forces.

> [It] is a policy of involvement in world affairs. It is not that we have no views, or that we wish to be available as mediators and arbitrators if the opportunity occurs. Such a role can be an honourable one, but it is not the major role of non-aligned states. Our role arises from the fact that we have very definite international policies of our own, but ones which are separate from and independent of those of either of the power blocs. By non-alignment we are saying to the Big Powers that we also belong to this planet. We are asserting the right of small, or militarily weaker, nations to determine their own policies in their own interests, and to have an influence on

world affairs ... Non-alignment does not imply agreement on major issues, it is simply a statement by a particular country that it will determine its policies for itself according to its own judgements about its needs and the merits of a case. It is thus a refusal to be party to any permanent diplomatic or military identification with the Great Powers; it is a refusal to take part in any alliances, or to allow any military bases by the Great Powers.

The threat to smaller nations, Nyerere claimed, came not from the military but from the economic powers of big states: 'At every point ... we find our real freedom to make economic, social and political choices is being jeopardised by our need for economic development.' Thus he advised the movement to consider how it could help to strengthen non-alignment by economic cooperation among its members. 'This is the field in which we can really affect changes invulnerable to outside pressure. It is one which we can do something about if we work together.' The strength of the non-aligned movement, he argued, lay in its members' ability to help each other rather than waiting as individuals for help from the great powers which merely created obligations. 'The fundamental question is whether we recognise and accept that the progress of each member of the non-aligned countries depends on the progress of us all. For this is the truth which we reject at our peril.'

Results and reactions
The conference adopted the Lusaka Declaration on Peace, Independence, Development, Cooperation and Democratisation of International Relations.[11] Its themes were colonialism, racism, economic criticism of the developed countries, and the formulation of measures toward economic self-reliance within the ldcs. A preliminary meeting of non-aligned Foreign Ministers at Dar es Salaam subsequently adopted a report of the Economic and Technological Cooperation Committee of the Lusaka conference which criticised rich nations for not sufficiently aiding the poor. It also noted 'with profound disappointment' that progress in the Second Development Decade had commanded universal support only on the level of generalities, and deplored 'the lack of seriousness of purpose evident in the unwillingness of developed nations to implement measures to facilitate increased absorption of products from developing countries'. The real threat to the independence of the non-aligned, it was agreed, came from their 'iniquitous' economic relationships with developed coun-

tries. The report called for policies of self-reliance to be adopted, and for the 'fostering of economic relationships among the developing nations at all levels'.[12]

The West did not appreciate the change of direction taking place in the non-aligned movement at Lusaka. Nyerere's plan to convert non-alignment into a 'trade union of the have-nots' was mentioned in its press, but was considered unlikely to materialise. The Soviet Union agreed that the non-aligned should seek to achieve cohesion in their approach, but an article in *Izvestia* suggested that this might best be achieved by adopting an anti-Western or anti-imperialist theme.

Thus the Lusaka conference, reluctantly entered into by many ldcs, had developed a new and important economic theme which was to be further developed at the next non-aligned conference at Algiers.

ALGIERS 1973   FOURTH SUMMIT CONFERENCE (Theme: the new international economic order)

The Foreign Ministers were late in preparing an agenda for this meeting as there was again dispute about which countries were qualified to attend. The disagreement was over the Libyan proposal to exclude any countries harbouring foreign military bases. Colonel Gadaffi of Libya implied that Cuba's Fidel Castro had no business attending the non-aligned summit because he was, in his opinion, aligned, having accepted 'the domination of Russia'; the Libyans also argued that non-alignment should be provided with a formal charter. These proposals were supported by radicals like Somalia and Burundi, but India, Nigeria, Morocco and Sierra Leone felt that they would prove unworkable and divisive owing to the diverse membership of the non-aligned movement. It was finally agreed that the criteria for membership of the twelve-year-old non-aligned movement would be non-participation in military pacts with the great powers.

The conference
The growing self-confidence of Third World Heads of State was clearly evident at Algiers. After the meeting India's Mrs Gandhi said: 'there exists a far greater feeling of ability among the non-aligned nations to do something, whereas in the past there was something of an element of helplessness to implement the decisions and declarations, especially in the economic sphere.'

One of the main new elements to emerge in the conference was a growing awareness that ldcs had a certain leverage for obtaining developed country concessions through their control of essential raw materials. The OPEC action over oil later in 1973 emphasised the significance of, for example, a statement by President Kaunda made at Algiers:

The Third World must not lay itself open to the uncontrolled exploitation of its natural resources . . . and cannot therefore continue to support world demand at the present rate of industrialisation . . . We must therefore not pursue policies in mineral and oil production which, while yielding high returns in foreign exchange, are sure to result in mines being exhausted and oil wells drying up in the near future, leaving the producers without the means of sustaining economic and social development. We must seriously coordinate our efforts in the conservation and larger utilisation of the valuable resources of the Third World.'[13]

Results — The New International Economic Order
The Algiers conference endorsed the Action Programme for Economic Cooperation[14] agreed in August 1972 by the Third Conference of Ministers of the Non-aligned Movement held at Georgetown, Guyana. This specified major areas of cooperation among non-aligned and other ldcs — trade, industry and transport; technology and technological assistance; financial and monetary cooperation; international cooperation for economic development — and assigned responsibility for working on each to certain nations.

The Action Programme reflected a link between the Non-aligned Movement and the Group of 77; it recommended that non-aligned countries should act as a catalytic force in the Group, in order to increase the effectiveness and solidarity of the ldcs. In essence the Action Programme was a restatement of proposals put to UNCTAD III at Santiago in 1972 by the Group of 77, and further emphasised at Georgetown. These reiterated that nothing could be expected from the developed countries, so that the ldcs must cooperate among themselves; indeed this feeling was borne out by their disappointment with the results of the Second Development Decade.

The Algiers conference also issued an Economic Declaration[15] which reflected the ldcs' perceptions of their economic problems. It dealt with 14 main issues which ranged over an extremely broad political, economic and cultural spectrum.

The main result of the conference at Algiers was that the framework of the New International Economic Order was outlined for the first

time. The ideas which were to crystallise into Third World demands
for a NIEO were put forward in the Action Programme together with
the Economic Declaration. Collective self-reliance, increased sovereignty over natural resources, and national control over private
foreign investment in ldcs were emphasised. Furthermore, an ldc
meeting to decide strategy concerning primary products was called for
— 'The Heads of State or Government ... considered it advisable
that a conference of developing countries be convened on commodities with a view to developing an effective strategy for restructuring
world trade and improving their bargaining power.'[16]

Algiers led directly to the UN Sixth Special Session on development
and cooperation which is the subject of the next chapter. 'The Heads
of State or Government ... invite the Secretary-General of the United
Nations to convene a special session of the General Assembly at a high
political level devoted exclusively to the problems of development, including the revitalisation of structure and the implementation of the
goals and objectives of the International Development Strategy.'

COLOMBO 1976   FIFTH SUMMIT CONFERENCE (Theme: economic cooperation)

At the Ministerial Conference of non-aligned nations in Dakar in
February 1975, the non-aligned further developed the philosophy gov-
erning their actions, and formulated a set of proposals to present to
the developed countries. They also produced the most comprehensive
ideological statement to date concerning the movement towards a New
International Economic Order.[17] This was based on Raul Prebisch's
centre–periphery analysis,[18] and reflected the increasing acceptance of
Marxist and dependence theories of underdevelopment. The centre–
periphery concept applies at all scales from the micro to the macro,
from the national to the world space economy; the latter is at issue
here. The argument is that rich capitalist country development implies
the colonial and neo-colonial exploitation of the periphery, in this case
the underdeveloped countries. Underdevelopment can only be understood historically as part of the capitalist system. An international
division of labour prevents the full development of peripheral areas,
which are forced to adapt to the needs of the centre; the Third World
provides the rich countries with raw materials and cheap labour. Thus

underdevelopment is an essential part of capitalist development. The non-aligned ministers at Dakar proposed to establish a 'Solidarity Fund' to support resource cartels on the OPEC model. The question of debt was also raised, and the need for an international equivalent of 'self-reliance' was noted — something new in conventional development planning. The main provisions of the Dakar Declaration were incorporated into the final resolution of the Second General Conference of the UN Industrial Development Organisation held in Lima in March 1975. The most important part of its Lima Declaration demanded a redistribution of world industrial growth to enable the Third World to possess 25 per cent of the world's industrial capacity by the year 2000. In August the non-aligned Foreign Ministers met and produced the Lima Programme for Mutual Assistance and Solidarity. This endorsed the results of the Dakar conference, the Lima UNIDO conference and the Third World 'North–South Dialogue' in Paris. Included in it was a section entitled 'Stategy to Strengthen International Peace and Security and to Intensify Solidarity and Mutual Assistance among Non-aligned Countries', which was really a plan of action for strengthening cooperation, solidarity and efficiency among ldcs.

The conference
Thus the Colombo conference of 1976 took place at a time of intensive international negotiations on a wide range of economic issues. Preparations for UNCTAD IV were under way, and the conference which began in 1975 on International Economic Cooperation (the North–South dialogue) faced serious problems. The emphasis on cooperation in the resolution of the ldcs' economic problems was clearly the theme of Colombo; politics was sterile if it did not lead to economic hope and betterment, and in the ultimate, to true economic independence. To some extent the non-aligned movement emerged at Colombo as resembling a 'trade union of the Third World'.

Despite many disagreements between radical and moderate states, in the end a sense of unity prevailed at Colombo. Full membership of the non-aligned movement was still denied to states that were in alliance with foreign powers, but at Colombo guest seats were provided for Portugal, the Philippines and Rumania. For the first time the movement had created formal links with allies of the Great Powers, and it might have moved further in this direction but for India, which feared a precedent which might have led to the admission of Pakistan. Since Algiers, Communist membership of the non-aligned movement has increased, largely as a result of the outcome of the Vietnam war.

Results

The final agreed Joint Economic and Political Declaration was tougher and more comprehensive than the 1975 Dakar Declaration or the Lima Programme for Mutual Assistance and Solidarity. In it the West was blamed for the deadlock in the North–South dialogue in that its lack of progress was seen as reflecting a lack of political will on the part of the developed countries to effect substantial change in their economic relations with less developed countries. Ldcs were called on to mobilise their national resources as an effective weapon, following the OPEC action on oil. The Declaration confirmed associations with the Group of 77, recognising that

'the economic content of the non-aligned movement has influenced and in turn has been influenced by the articulate and dynamic organisation of the Group of 77. The non-aligned movement shall continue to maintain and strengthen its solidarity with the Group of 77 which has today emerged as a real force of countervailing authority. The non-aligned countries emphasise the highly constructive role of the Group of 77 in the negotiations for advancing the cause of the developing countries, particularly in the establishment of the New International Economic Order.'[19]

The Declaration did not really contain new proposals, but its language was more combative and aggressive than hitherto in the non-aligned movement. It represented a hardening of the original Sri Lankan draft, which had been more conciliatory; remnants of this in the final draft referred to the more enlightened attitude of some developed countries like those of Scandinavia, and reflected the general view that there was still time, although this was limited, for cooperation with the developed countries. In this the non-aligned resisted efforts by the Communists, particularly Cuba, to define the capitalist West as an enemy to be destroyed. In addition to the Political and the Economic Declaration an Action Programme for Economic Cooperation[20] emerged from the conference. Its main aims were to be effected through measures dealing with raw materials, trade, finance, industry and economic order.

Colombo produced for the movement a general institutional agreement to convert its 17-member coordinating committee into a permanent and enlarged Coordinating Bureau based at the United Nations headquarters in New York. The proposal called for monthly meetings of the bureau at the level of permanent representatives to the UN and at least one annual meeting at foreign minister level. A further and most interesting proposal was that of setting up a non-aligned News Agencies' Pool to disseminate Third World news.[21] It was argued that the Western news agencies tended to report such news in a distorted and incomplete manner. The debate about this and its possible effects on press freedom continues to date.

HAVANA 1979 SIXTH SUMMIT CONFERENCE (Theme: non-alignment itself)

In June 1979 the 25 members of the Coordinating Bureau of the non-aligned movement met in Colombo, Sri Lanka, to prepare an agenda for the Sixth Summit. The issues which preoccupied them were primarily political, and very divisive. The two main ones concerned the Egyptian–Israeli peace treaty and the establishment of the legitimacy of the Kampuchean delegation. After five days of debate the meeting agreed to compromise. The Arab states failed to have Egypt suspended from the movement, the bureau finding that the matter was 'beyond its competence'. With regard to Kampuchea, the bureau accepted the credentials of the Pol Pot rather than those of the Heng Samrin group, but without allowing its members to speak; at the summit meeting which followed Kampuchea's seat was kept empty.

The conference

The non-aligned foreign ministers met in Havana in early September 1979, just before the meeting of Heads of State. Seven new member states were admitted to the movement — Iran, the Patriotic Front, Bolivia, Grenada, Nicaragua, Surinam and, at last, Pakistan.

The dominant issue at the conference — non-alignment itself — had already emerged at Colombo through discussion of Kampuchea and Arab opposition to Egypt in the light of the Camp David agreement. Other central political events were equally relevant to it — Cuba's role in Africa, the Somali–Ethiopia conflict, the Western Saharan dispute, unrest in Nicaragua, Vietnam's policies in South-east Asia, US publicity of Soviet combat troops in Cuba. These all raised the question of great power involvement in the affairs of the non-aligned, while equally important were the attempts of Cuba (the host country) to direct the non-aligned movement towards the ideology of the Soviet Union.

The revised draft of the summit declaration submitted by Cuba was couched along clear pro-Soviet lines. It referred to several major and controversial issues: (a) current political events, expressed in Marxist terminology but criticised on this count by the general view of the committees which discussed the draft; (b) measures in terms of trade, aid, transfer of technology, the international monetary system; (c) OPEC and the supply of oil to the ldcs; (d) an international fund to aid ldcs, the donors being the dcs and the oil exporting countries.

Results and comment
Havana is too recent an event for any valid assessment of the implications of its results, so that only cursory comment may be made.

Castro's pro-Soviet stance — so critical in future because of his leadership of the non-aligned group for the next three years, and with Cuba as the host country for UNCTAD VI in 1982 — was very strongly evident, and dominated much of the conference proceedings. Those countries opposed to it found their most effective spokesman in Tanzania's President Nyerere. His speech of 7 September argued that the non-aligned movement was a progressive movement, but not a movement of progressive states. 'We have socialists here, but we are not a movement of socialist states. From the very beginning, membership has included states which claim an ideological commitment to socialism, those which aspire to build capitalism, and some who claim to be neither socialist nor capitalist.'[22] India's Foreign Minister argued along the same lines: 'We cannot have one foot in non-alignment and another in alignment ... We must not allow ourselves, even unwittingly, to subserve the ulterior ends of outside powers and act in a manner inconsistent with the fundamental principles of our movement.'[23]

In the end the final Summit Declaration stressed the 'authentic, independent and non-bloc factor'[24] of the non-aligned movement, while still retaining much of Cuba's anti-imperialist views. In the economic sphere the most important section called for guaranteed oil supplies to the ldcs from the oil producers.

Political issues and idealogical disputes were evident and dominant at Havana. Nevertheless there was near unanimity for a new international economic order, and a clear stress on the need for self-reliance by the movement. These two issues were enough to unite the diverse and divided non-aligned countries. Despite the difficulty of isolating its meaning, non-alignment is a concept with sufficient relevance to ldcs for it to endure. Since the early Belgrade conference, of all the countries present about half now have different heads of state, but all continue to describe themselves as non-aligned.

4 The Sixth and Seventh Special Sessions of the United Nations 1974 and 1975

THE SIXTH SPECIAL SESSION GENERAL ASSEMBLY   1974

The dramatic quadrupling of petroleum prices in 1973 provided the immediate impetus for the Sixth Special Session. One leading Third World economist working in USA commented that while the US State Department believed that what was at stake was an increase in raw materials prices, what had to be faced was that the premises on which major post-war institutions like the World Bank and GATT were based were now crumbling away.[1] In view of its obvious importance OPEC is considered in the following chapter.

In February 1974 Algeria called for a special session of the UN General Assembly to consider the question of raw materials and trading relationships, in the light of the energy crisis. Its delegate to the UN, Mr Abdellatif Rahal, gave the Secretary-General, Dr Kurt Waldheim, a letter suggesting that the special session should define a new economic relationship between the industrial and developing nations. Through the letter President Boumedienne of Algeria gave support to a French proposal for a world energy conference under UN auspices, but argued that it should be in the form of an emergency session of the General Assembly and should deal not only with energy sources but with all raw materials. He acted in his capacity as Chairman of the summit conference of non-aligned nations held at Algiers in September 1973, since the idea of such a session first arose in that movement (see Chapter 3). The timing of the approach came as a surprise to most non-aligned nations but they soon expressed support for the meeting. It became apparent that Boumedienne had acted quickly in order to counter both President Nixon's initiative in calling a conference of major oil-consuming countries in Washington on 11 February, and the French proposal. Boumedienne argued that any discussion of petroleum and other primary products should be kept within the UN framework. Moreover he sought an action programme aimed at ensuring that ldcs achieved a more equitable return for their raw materials, and a 'fair and lasting' trade balance; as well as this, reforms in the international monetary system were sought in order to give ldcs what they regarded as adequate decision-making power.

A majority of 70 of the 135 UN members, including OPEC and EEC countries, had endorsed the special session by February, so its date was set for 9 April; USA and the Soviet Union did not respond positively.

Group preparations

The less developed countries
In March the foreign ministers of 17 non-aligned ldcs met in Algiers to prepare for the Sixth Special Session. They produced a draft declaration, but although many ldcs (particularly the poorest of them) were hard hit by the new oil prices, it made no mention of the energy crisis and the effects of these increases. The ldc intended action programme called for 'the establishment and improvement of ... producers' associations and joint marketing arrangements among the ldcs to defend the producers of exportable primary commodities'. President Boumedienne expressed his view: 'current international conditions have conferred particular significance upon the joint action of the oil-producing countries, which, in exercise of their sovereignty, are undertaking the mobilisation of their domestic resources to place them at the service of development and of the advancement of their populations.' He argued that what was needed was 'a new system of relations ... the establishment of the equilibrium which has now become imperative and which the international community has been seeking in vain for many years through the efforts of the ldcs'.[2]

In effect the ldcs sought from the Special Session endorsement of the New International Economic Order. Their Declaration wanted the Assembly to declare 'It is not possible to achieve an even and balanced development of the international community under the existing international economic system. The gap between the developed and the developing countries continues to widen in a system that was established at a time when most of the developing countries did not even exist as independent states and which, by all these elements, per-petuates inequality.'[3] It contained many requests, including a guarantee 'of preferential and non-reciprocal treatment to developing countries in all fields of international economic cooperation', and the 'establishment of a just and equitable relationship between the prices of raw materials, primary products, manufactured and semi-manufactured goods exported by developing countries and the prices of manufactures, capital goods and equipment imported by them, with the aim of improving their terms of trade'. It asserted that nations have the right to control, develop and nationalise resources, and urged that poor countries be allocated foreign aid and guaranteed preferential treatment in trade and monetary arrangements. The declaration referred to such issues as 'the most important problems facing the world community', and consequently proposed yet another special session in 1975, to deal with economic problems.

The Organisation of Petroleum Exporting Countries (OPEC)

In April Algeria prepared a draft on behalf of the Arab states in which it was noted that they were entitled to exploit their own natural re-sources as they wished, but were prepared both to invest in the developed countries and to help the less developed.

At an OPEC meeting in Geneva 12 oil producing states decided to set up a fund to help the ldcs, particularly the poorest of them. They were divided on the amount of their contributions, but Iran had offered $2 billion (UK) through the World Bank, and Kuwait had promised to increase substantially its contributions to a Fund for Arab Economic Development with a commitment to other ldcs.

The developed countries

The EEC countries endorsed Algeria's call for the Special Session, and of the great powers USA alone rejected an invitation to confer with the smaller nations in planning for it; the US delegate, John A. Scali, claimed that his country's attitude could be described as 'constructive waiting' and one of concern that the Assembly's actions should not hamper efforts outside the UN to deal with the energy crisis nor inter-fere with future meetings on trade and monetary arrangements.

Reports at the time suggested that the initial reaction to the oil price increase was to form another bloc to oppose it. The Nixon administra-tion found it difficult to accept that there might be a better solution, and became annoyed with the European countries when they showed some reluctance to support its plan for a joint counter-attack.

The special session
The President of the previous regular General Assembly session, Ambassador Leopoldo Bennites of Ecuador, was elected President, while Fereydoun Hoveyda, head of the Iranian UN mission was elected without opposition as Chairman of the only working committee to function at the session, that dealing with raw materials and development.

The subject of the conference — raw materials and development — was debated with unusual seriousness by both the developed and less developed countries, largely because of the oil crisis, the deepening world-wide recession, continuing inflation creating higher prices for ldcs in paying for their imports, and massive surpluses accumulated by the oil producers. The Sixth Session attempted to draw up a blue-print for future trading in commodities. Ldcs were determined to ensure they did not continue selling their raw materials at artificially low prices fixed by the industrialised countries, and the conference highlighted the divergence of views on what constituted a just international economic order. The dcs sought to demonstrate that the energy problem was at the root of the economic crisis, arguing that increases in oil prices led to inflation which in turn led to recession and world-wide hardship. For ldcs the main issue was the relationship between the prices of goods and commodities in international exchange. Gamani Corea of Sri Lanka became the new UNCTAD Secretary-General on 5 April and urged ldcs to evolve a strategy for this. He suggested arrangements for buffer stocks based on several commodities and supported by a central fund, and argued for the provision of long-term loans by oil-exporting countries to allow those buffer stocks to be established. 'If these ... were jointly financed through a central fund those loans would enjoy a high degree of security, since they would have holdings of real assets as collateral, whose value would keep pace with inflation and would also reflect changes in currency exchange rates.'[4] He suggested as another possibility for financing such a commodity-stabilisation programme, a 'small levy on international trade in general'.

Attention is now paid to group positions as expressed by participants.

The less developed countries
The main issue for the Third World concerned the despair, especially among its poorest countries, resultant upon oil price increases. According to a World Bank report[5] prepared for the session ldcs were

estimated to be paying between $10000 and $12000 million more for imported oil in 1974, and would require additional financial assistance of some $6600 million in 1974 and $9000 million in 1975. This report clearly confirmed the magnitude and immediacy of their financial difficulties. Of 97 UN ldcs the World Bank listed 12 — representing over 1000 million people — which it considered to be in particular distress: Bangladesh, Bolivia, Pakistan, Ethiopia, India, Kenya, Mali, Sri Lanka, Sudan, Tanzania, Uganda and Zaire.

The 34-nation Commonwealth group at the UN was resuscitated after its hitherto frequent discussions had been suspended in 1970 as a result of British policy towards Zimbabwe–Rhodesia, and the Indian External Affairs Minister, Mr Swaran Singh disclosed that Dr Waldheim was to play a central role in persuading oil-rich states and other affluent countries to set up an emergency fund.

China played a prominent part in the Special Session. Her Deputy Premier, Deng Xiauping, argued that 'the socialist camp is no longer in existence',[6] the Western bloc is disintegrating, and the world now consists of the super powers, the developed countries, and the Third World ldcs — among whom he squarely placed China. An editorial in the *Peking People's Daily* commented that 'the oil battle has . . . made the Third World peoples aware of their own might. They have become increasingly aware that what has been achieved with oil should and can be achieved with other raw materials.'[7] Indeed a particularly aggressive stance in favour of higher prices were taken by ldc suppliers of certain irreplaceable minerals. They discussed the possibility of collective action in such strategic materials, although it was appreciated that lack of political unity might be divisive despite the example of OPEC unity on oil prices since 1970 regardless of its political divisions. Two of the Copper Exporters' Council for example, Zambia and Chile, had broken off diplomatic relations with each other after the Allende coup in Chile.

The session debated a list of 25 ldc principles for the establishment of 'A New International Economic Order' accompanied by an 80-point 'action programme'. This asserted the right of sovereignty over natural resources, argued that compensation for nationalised property should be determined by the nationalising country, encouraged cartels, and called for a link between the price of Third World exports and manufactured imports to replace the current free trade system so as to improve ldc terms of trade.

The Organisation of Petroleum Exporting Countries (OPEC)
President Boumedienne of Algeria dismissed the oil price increases as

'ridiculously small'[8] and attributed the shortages of such raw materials to overconsumption by the rich countries. He urged the ldcs to nationalise their primary resources, and to set up new cartels to force higher commodity prices upon the consumers. The Iranian Finance Minister, Jamshid Amouzegar, warned that if inflation continued then oil prices would go up again in October, while his government accused Dr Kissinger of 'gross misrepresentation' in the remarks he made about rising oil prices during the debate in the UN General Assembly. Iran declared that the main reason for the high price of oil was not OPEC action, but the level of taxation over the years on petroleum products in the dcs: 'In some cases revenues secured from taxation on a barrel of crude are four to nine times the revenue of exporting nations.'[9] It suggested that another main reason was the 'exorbitant profits' reaped by the major oil companies. Iraq, Saudi Arabia and Kuwait also justified their oil price rises and blamed the dcs for the resultant economic problems. They ignored the Iranian proposal for a fund to aid the poorest ldcs, and advised the developed countries to improve their assistance to them. Saudi Arabia was the most conciliatory towards the industrialised countries and was prepared to discuss the international economic situation, including energy and prices, with them. Nevertheless its spokesman Sheik Yamani called on the developed countries to bear 'the greater part' of the responsibilities for extending aid to the ldcs.

The developed countries

The USA sought to keep major negotiations outside the session. It was concerned that the ldcs would use their voting strength to approve new principles, or even new machinery, in order to alter the pattern of commodity and trade arrangements and thus threaten the existing economic balance. Dr Kissinger warned them that the USA would not respond to the 'politics of pressure and threats', and argued that 'no nation or group of nations can gain by pushing its claims beyond the limits that sustain world economic growth'.[10] However he pledged the USA to 'a major effort in support of development'. with increased assistance in several areas. He emphasised that the issue should not be seen in terms of confrontation between rich and poor: '. . . If the weak resort to pressure, they will do so at the risk of world prosperity and thus provoke despair', and argued that the present session should 'strengthen our commitment to find cooperative solutions within the appropriate forums such as the World Bank, the IMF, GATT, and the world food and population conferences'[11] He referred to the problem areas in which action was called for: emergency supplies of raw

materials, food and population growth, aid for the poorest, full use of
science and technology, improvement of the trade, monetary and investment system. At the last minute, on 1 May, the USA proposed a
$4000 million relief programme in an effort to provide 'a quick,
effective and pragmatic answer' to the economic crisis. However, this
programme was brushed aside without discussion, and instead delegates approved the ldc package; they argued that there was no time
for discussion and that this should be postponed until the July session
of the Economic and Social Council. The USA then withdrew its plan.

Most Western European nations confirmed that despite the damage
to their economies they would maintain and increase aid to the most
badly affected countries. The EEC offered support for the new aid
fund to help the poorest ldcs; it was not committed to any specific
amount of financial assistance (though it had suggested a $500 million
contribution to a fund of $2000 million) nor to the support of any
particular project. The British preference was for the new soft loan
fund proposed by the Iranians. The West German Foreign Minister,
Mr Scheel, stressed the EEC's support of its associated states (the
Lomé Convention), while the French Foreign Minister, Mr Jobert,
pleaded for new commodity agreements, particularly with regard to
oil and grains.

Results
The Sixth Special Session closed on 2 May 1974. After 13 weeks it had
agreed on a 'Declaration on the establishment of a New International
Economic Order' and a 'Programme of Action', which included
special measures to help the countries which had been hardest hit by
such recent trends as the rise in the price of oil. The conference's most
specific recommendations were those dealing with the poorest countries, the lldcs. The UN was to launch an emergency operation to
help them maintain their essential imports over the next year; the
conference called on the developed countries and other potential con-
tributors to announce their aid commitments by 15 June. A decision
was taken to set up a special fund under UN auspices with voluntary
contributions to provide emergency relief and development assistance
to start by 1 January 1975.

However, both the above documents were the work of the ldcs, and
amendments put forward by the USA, the EEC and the Soviet Union
were rejected. The USA, the EEC and Japan opposed the key provisions in the Declaration which upheld the right of countries to nationalise their properties without providing compensation, and criticised

the Action Programme's proposals for emergency relief, arguing that more than promises were required. The developed countries did not vote on the final resolution since they were outnumbered. John Scali, the US delegate, rejected the idea that the result was a consensus: 'To label some of these highly controversial conclusions as agreed is not only idle, it is self deceiving . . . the steamroller is not the vehicle for solving vital complex problems';[12] the USA regarded the session as both a confrontation between rich and poor and as a rallying point for anti-American feeling.[13]

The Sixth Session may indeed have displayed confrontation more than cooperation, but it did allow the important issues of a new world economic order to be raised, and marked the first formulation of these at the UN by the less developed countries.

THE SEVENTH SPECIAL SESSION GENERAL ASSEMBLY 1975

The Seventh Special Session on development and cooperation was convened in September 1975 as a follow-up to the Sixth Special Session held on raw materials and development in 1974. Both were the only special sessions in the United Nations' 30-year history to be primarily concerned with economic matters. Although the issues concerned had not changed since 1974, the economic and political climate had. In early 1974 there had been a commodity boom, and the influence of 'producer power' was strong after OPEC price rises in that year. By the time of the Seventh Session the international economy was in its deepest recession since the 1930s, and commodity prices were low. The formation and effective operation of OPEC had also forced the developed countries towards a realisation of the grievances and power of the Third World. OPEC's ministerial meeting in Vienna on 24 September decided that oil price rises would be influenced by the results of the Seventh Session. There was also an awareness in the West that it could no longer realistically hope for the collapse of Third World or OPEC solidarity, and this necessitated some new thinking on its part. President Giscard d'Estaing had attempted to initiate an 'energy dialogue' at Paris in April, but this proved abortive. In May the OECD issued a Declaration on Developing Countries following a highly conciliatory communiqué from the board of the US-dominated International Energy Agency.

Solidarity between oil producers and non-oil producing ldcs had been reaffirmed in a summit meeting of non-aligned foreign ministers at Lima in August 1975. This led to the adoption of proposals to set up a multi-billion dollar 'solidarity fund' to finance commodity buffer stocks; this was to be operated by raw material producer associations through a coordinating mechanism to link groups into a potential 'cartel of cartels' and by means of guidelines provided for the treatment of foreign investment capital.

The ldcs recommended six topics for the Seventh Special Session to consider: trade and aid, monetary reform, science and technology, industrialisation, food and agriculture, and the reorganisation of UN economic and social programmes.

The special session
This is considered largely in terms of group positions as expressed by participants.

The developed countries
At the Seventh Session the USA changed its approach towards the Third World. It had not endorsed any major documents of the Group of 77, such as the Declaration on the New International Economic Order, the Charter of Economic Rights and Duties of States, or the Lima Declaration. Dr Kissinger now sought to move away from confrontation, although he had considerable opposition for this new approach within the Ford Administration. He was supported by the new US Representative at the United Nations, Daniel Moynihan, and by Charles Robinson, the Secretary of State for Economic Affairs. Opposition to his conciliatory line came from the Treasury Department Secretary, William Simon. In order to avoid having to depend on the Treasury Department, and because of uncertainty over Congress' response, Dr Kissinger directed that most US proposals be framed so that they would not require new legislation, and thus could be implemented under the Trade Reform Act of 1974. Thus the USA participated in preparations for the Seventh Special Session whereas in the Sixth its representatives had boycotted the planning meetings on the grounds that they had not been adequately consulted.

The proposals put forward by USA offered a number of suggestions to promote development, and attempted to encourage continued negotiations with the Third Word. Kissinger's proposed strategy for development concentrated on five specific areas: (a) Poor countries must be assured of basic economic security, which meant cushioning them against violent commodity price fluctuations which would drastically cut their export earnings. But price stabilisation was opposed because it would mean 'severe restrictions on production or price levels which could stimulate substitutes and thereby work to the long-range disadvantage of producers'.[14] (b) Developing countries required much more aid than they could ever obtain bilaterally; acceleration of their economic growth would require something like $40 000 million. The solution proposed was to provide investment, and Kissinger urged the Third World to provide a more hospitable climate for foreign and multinational corporations which could supply the financing they required for development. (c) Dr Kissinger proposed to lower trading barriers, in order to give special consideration to the products of developing countries. He stated that the USA was ready to join other nations in providing greater concessions to the manufacturers of the ldcs. However he emphasised that the developing countries also had an obligation not to use barriers to deprive other countries of goods which they needed; he contended that the developing nations had never been willing to concede this. (d) He offered to cooperate in establishing a number of buffer stocks in various commodities, especially food. Such reserves would both improve the commodity price market and prevent shortages. (e) The plan proposed increasing the Third World's influence in the World Bank and the IMF.

A closer examination of the US proposals led many observers[15] to conclude that the USA had not adopted a change in attitude, but merely a new tactic — a method of avoiding confrontation. This would serve also to quieten the radical states among the ldcs, and would deprive the Third World of its more effective weapons, such as forming new raw material cartels and threatening to repudiate debt obligations.

Nevertheless the US initiative certainly altered the mood of the session. Even more radical Third World states were enthusiastic, one spokesman describing the US speech as 'a very good beginning; a very positive statement deserving of study'.[16] The Algerian Foreign Minister, Abdelazis Bouteflika, the leader of the radical states and elected President of the Session said 'It is clear that confrontation cannot but be hurtful to everyone ... It is the common criticism which demands that we search for effective solutions'.[17] 'We are speaking to one another, we are no longer barking at one another' Foreign Minister Gamal Mohammed Ahmed of the Sudan informed the Session.[18]

The other OECD countries generally supported the US change of stance. Japan and West Germany represented the most uncompromising dissidents of the developed countries. The Japanese delegate urged the strengthening of the free trade system, warning that the basic problems of the poor could not be solved by 'a mechanical and arbitrary redistribution of wealth'.[19] West Germany came down categorically against the indexation principle of tying the price of raw materials to that of manufactured goods — one of the ldcs' main demands. Foreign Minister Hans-Dietrich Genscher told the Special Session 'The task of finding a fair index formula is insoluble even in theory. In practice, any attempt to enforce the index price would be followed by a flood of government controls.'[20] He insisted that the aim of increasing the commercial earnings of the ldcs must be done through the workings of the free market 'by increasing productivity and hence profits, by boosting sales and ultimately by a determined policy of diversification'.[21]

Mr Genscher identified his country with the new joint European approach outlined by the Italian Foreign Minister, Signor Mariano Rumor on 1 September. This aimed to build on the concessions already offered to 46 ldcs under the EEC's Lomé Convention signed early in 1975. It included provisions for stabilising export earnings from raw materials by the ldcs, increasing their overall foreign exchange earnings, and avoiding excessive price fluctuations (the Stabex scheme).

The Scandinavians, particularly Sweden, adopted a position closer to the ldcs and generally to the left of the EEC. Sweden, at that time the only country meeting the target of 0.7 per cent of GNP as official development assistance, proposed an international agreement to write off, or at least substantially reduce the debt burden of the world's poorest countries. Its Minister of State, Carl Lidbom, informed the Session that his government would write off Swedish credits to the least developed countries and the Most Severely Affected countries, and in future all official Swedish development assistance would be in the form of grants.

The Soviet Union and China clashed at the Seventh Session, the former accusing China of seeking to use developing countries as stepping stones to world domination. The Chinese Foreign Trade Minister, Li Qiang, warned the Third World against being taken in by the USSR while trying to deal with the USA: 'Developing countries', he said, 'must guard against the danger of letting the tiger in through the back door, while repulsing the wolf at the front gate.'[22]

The less developed countries
The session was opened by the Algerian President of the Assembly

who presented the Third World programme for radical economic change and the New International Economic Order, based on the formulations of the previous special session. Gamani Corea, the Secretary-General of UNCTAD, set out the problems facing the meeting. The central issues on which ldcs sought to focus were the need to restructure world commodity trade, the alleviation of Third World debt and the strengthening of ldcs exports. The UNCTAD Secretariat proposals were for an integrated commodity programme to improve the prices and trading conditions of key raw material exports by the Third World. This involved a large common cash-pool to support the price level for 18 key commodities. On the question of setting aside specific aid targets for developed countries, the Group of 77 demanded a commitment of up to 0.7 per cent of GNPs by 1978. With regard to a link between aid and the creation of new IMF special drawing rights the group sought immediate action. It rejected the IMF view that current world liquidity was adequate, and demanded the early creation of more SDRs. India took the lead on the discussions on debt, where ldcs sought a moratorium for the most heavily indebted countries.

The major rift between the ldcs and the industrialised countries developed over indexation, during the final week of the conference. The position paper of the Group of 77 argued that the prices of ldc raw material exports should be tied to the prices of their imports from the developed countries, and it demanded insulation from the adverse effects of inflation in those countries. There was no mention of indexation in either the USA or the EEC position papers, and indeed the West Germans categorically denounced the whole idea. The European Community proposed international action to stabilise export earnings by improving the compensatory financing mechanisms of the IMF, and by introducing special measures to help the poorest countries.

Iran's Minister of the Interior, Jamshid Amouzegar, angered by US criticisms of the oil producing countries, responded sceptically to the new US proposals. These, he said 'may appear brilliant on paper but when and how they are implemented ... is the question'.[23]

Results

The final Seventh Special Session Resolution was adopted unanimously, first by a committee meeting in the early hours of 16 September and later in a plenary session of the General Assembly. It was however accompanied by a long statement of reservations by the US delegation, and by a shorter one from other countries including

Britain. Mr Jacob Myerson, the American representative, told the committee that 'the US cannot and does not accept any implication that the world is now embarked on the establishment of something called the New International Economic Order'.[24] He added a number of specific reservations on points in the resolution dealing with trade, aid and reform of the monetary system, and rejected 'indexing' and the target of 0.7 per cent of GNP set for official aid by the end of the decade. The reservations of the EEC were presented by Italy; Britain rejected the aid target, and reported that access to the British capital market must remain limited.

The resolution consisted of a preamble, an operative paragraph, and seven sections recommending specific measures. These sections concerned international trade, the transfer of resources from the rich to the poor countries, science and technology, industrialisation, food and agriculture, cooperation among the developing countries themselves, and the restructuring of the economic and social sectors of the UN system. The section on international trade called for a continuation and acceleration of negotiations and discussions which were taking place *inter alia* at UNCTAD and in the Multilateral Trade Negotiations under the General Agreement on Trade and Tariffs. There was no outright commitment to indexation, but there was a call for concerted efforts 'with a view to countermanding the adverse effects of inflation and thereby sustaining the real incomes'[25] of the ldcs. Neither was there full accord upon international commodity agreements, nor for a common fund to finance them; instead the resolution took note of these, and urged the developed countries to study them. The Group of 77 won a limited commitment to the achievement of the 0.7 per cent aid figure by 1980.

The Seventh Special Session clearly failed in its efforts to secure a New International Economic Order. But there was some commitment to further negotiations, and one major forum for this was to be the Conference on International Economic Cooperation (CIEC) which was convened in October 1975 at Paris.

5 The Organisation of Petroleum Exporting Countries

As with other organisations discussed in this book OPEC's history reflects a continuing record of differences and frustrations, but at the same time the retention of a prevailing theme of persistence and progress; and with more evident success because of its inherent wealth through developed resources.

The first major Arab oil congress was held at Cairo in 1959. Even there a difference of principle arose between two of its leading delegates, Sheik Abdulla al-Tariki, the Saudi-Arabian Director-General of Petroleum and Mineral Affairs, and Mr Emile Bustani, the Lebanese businessman and politician who frequently represented his country at inter-Arab oil meetings; the clash arose again in early 1960 at a meeting of the Arab League Economic Council. Mr Bustani proposed the formation of an Arab Development Bank to be financed by a percentage contribution from all Arab oil revenues. Sheik al-Tariki argued that this plan would improve the position of foreign interests and would weaken the bargaining power of the producing countries. He proposed a new Arab-owned pipeline from the Persian Gulf to the Mediterranean. Furthermore he argued that oil producing countries should concentrate on obtaining an increased share of profits, and should even consider 'Arabising' the various oil companies; his views were to prevail, and indeed to set the pattern for future policies among the oil producing states.

In August 1960 Mohammed Salman, a spokesman on oil for the Arab League, informed a press conference in New York that the Arab oil producing states hoped to form a company to build their own tankers and pipelines to extend their operations.[1] This matter was to be discussed at a petroleum conference of the Arab League in Beirut in October; the main subject under discussion was to be the coordination of certain petroleum activities by the oil producers.

Arab countries were becoming increasingly discontented with the low price of oil. It was expected that by October some of them might press for the renegotiation of certain older concessions awarded to the large international oil companies, or for supplemented subsidies to carry them through the current depressed oil market. In August 1960 Esso, followed by BP and Royal Dutch Shell, had reduced the prices of Middle East crude oil, without having consulted the producers. Sheik al-Tariki declared 'this constituted a violation of the spirit of the First Arab Petroleum Congress recommendation which requested the oil companies to hold consultations with the producing states before effecting alternatives in crude posted prices.'[2] The annual loss to Saudi Arabia he estimated as some $30 million; this was particularly critical for a country depending on oil for 98 per cent of its revenue, and at that time one with the lowest per capita income of any Arab country.

The '50–50' share was still the standard agreement in the Middle East. However al-Tariki said at a press conference in Caracas that the region intended following Venezuelan policies and would strive for a '60–40' agreement with the oil companies on profits. The Arabs' first task was to create a satisfactory organisation in the Middle East and then to convince its oil producers that the way to increase their income was by maintaining prices and not by increasing production at lower prices. The Venezuelan government was in agreement with the Middle East on the need for a three-part compact — the stabilisation of markets, the defence of prices and the conservation of resources — and would not sell to price-cutting companies. Antonio Araujo, its Ambassador to the United Arab Republic, said in August that he was trying to persuade Arab countries to keep the oil prices up in the face of cuts made by the oil companies which he accused of 'trying to split the Arab world from Venezuela'. In this way Venezuela proved to be an important influence in persuading the Middle East to pursue more aggressive policies.

At this stage Saudi Arabia was undoubtedly the Arab protagonist in trying to formulate a common attitude among its producers, as was Mohammed Salman the Director-General of Arab League petroleum affairs and Iraq's Oil Minister. The latter claimed that the recent lowering of prices was a political move in the East–West struggle, and rejected the argument that it was done in order to meet Soviet Union competition.

THE FORMATION OF OPEC   BAGHDAD 1960

In 1960 the Iraqi government invited Saudi Arabia, Kuwait, Qatar and Venezuela to an oil producers' conference in Baghdad. Two factors seem to have influenced Iraq in taking this initiative: Mr al-Tariki, visiting from Saudi Arabia, advised the Iraqis that oil producing countries should combine forces, while the Venezuelan Ambassador in Beirut, during the recent Arab foreign ministers' conference, discussed with Iraq the effect of the oil companies' decision to cut prices which was regarded as a very serious matter by the producers.

Delegates were officially invited only to discuss a unified policy with regard to the recent oil price cuts. However, Venezuela, Saudi Arabia and Iraq were determined that something more should be accomplished. Mohammed Salman, the Arab League Oil Director, suggested that the producing states reject the recent price cuts, but it was difficult to do this without nationalisation. The Saudis in particular were convinced that the price cuts resulted from the oil companies' desire to recoup losses from Venezuelan tax increases, by shifting their profits from production to refining and marketing, from which the producing countries received no share. The Iranians hitherto had evinced little desire to cooperate with the Arabs, but suddenly the Shah had begun to speak of breaking the 50–50 sharing agreements.

The Iraqi News Agency reported the results of the conference as follows: 'The five-nation conference of oil producers resolved that participating countries should take all measures to raise prices of crude oil to the same level as before the recent cuts were made by oil companies and to ask companies to maintain stable prices.'[3] The principle of consultation between participating countries and oil companies in future developments was adopted by the conference, and it was agreed that its delegations should investigate matters that might stabilise prices and limit production in a manner to guarantee producing countries a stable and regular income. By far the main result of the conference however was its decision to form OPEC, the Organisation of Petroleum Exporting Countries — for mutual consultation in order to unify and coordinate policy concerning oil production.

It was decided that any country producing a large quantity of crude oil could be a member of OPEC, subject to the unanimous agreement of the founding members. This was initially intended to permit entry to Libya and possibly a future independent Algeria. The 1979 members of OPEC are listed in Table 5.1. The OPEC secretariat was to meet in Baghdad in November to prepare for a second conference in Caracas in January 1961.

TABLE: 5.1
OPEC member states 1979

Algeria	Iran	Nigeria
Ecuador	Iraq	Qatar
Gabon	Kuwait	Saudi Arabia
Indonesia	Libya	United Arab Emirates
		Venezuela

SOURCE: *The Europa Yearbook,* 1979.

The five founder countries then represented the great majority of the world's oil exporters. However they were not as influential as might have been supposed since there was at the time a large world oil surplus. Nor were their individual interests identical. Venezuela and Saudi Arabia for instance, were concerned to restrict production in order to maintain prices; Iraq and the others, on the other hand, were increasing their sales and interested in getting a greater share of profits from crude oil production, and some share in profits from marketing and from refining in their territories.

CONSOLIDATION AND CONFLICT

From 1960 to the present time OPEC has extended its activities and actions through a series of meetings and negotiations and in the face both of internal stresses and problems which have arisen out of its relationships with the oil consumer nations. This process is briefly reviewed under appropriate headings.

Its second meeting at Caracas early in 1961 was concerned with plans to obtain increased royalties from the western oil companies in the Middle East, in order to compensate for losses caused by price cuts on the world oil market; a committee was set up to negotiate the revision of existing royalty agreements. At Tehran, after a postponement because of a political dispute between Iraq and Kuwait, its third meeting recommended consideration of 'appropriate increases' in its share of oil profits, and its member countries were asked to report back within two months on steps to restore prices to 'justified' levels. This general line of action was pursued at the fourth and fifth conferences with demands being formulated for higher crude oil posted prices, revision of the royalty payment situation and alterations in the tax treatment of a proportion of marketing expenses.

OPEC's basic aim during this early period was to oppose the oil companies on this particular price battle, and to formulate jointly a rational price structure to guide its long-term price policy. In the first part of this aim it succeeded. It also negotiated a standard form of agreement whereby, with the exception of Iraq which never ratified the negotiated settlement with the Iraq Petroleum Company, all companies came to operate under the same broad tax formula. *The Financial Times'* comment on OPEC's development by 1963 was that it 'has done some excellent work in the collection of information and in the coordination of the basic strategy of the oil-producing governments. But in terms of wringing major concessions from the oil companies it has little or nothing to show.'[4]

By the end of 1967 Iran, Libya, Abu Dhabi and Indonesia had joined OPEC, but a number of rifts had emerged among its members. Perhaps the most important was when Iran, Venezuela and Indonesia disregarded one of OPEC's main principles whereby its member countries should not benefit from each other's problems. When Arab countries first banned all exports of oil and later reduced this to an embargo on 'aggressive' states after the 1967 Middle East war, these three countries increased their petroleum exports to fill the gap.

OPEC EXTENDS ITS DEMANDS

In a 'declaratory statement of outstanding importance' issued at Vienna in July 1968 OPEC launched an attempt to revise the existing contractual arrangements with foreign oil companies. It suggested the following recommendations as a basis for a unified petroleum policy: governments should develop hydro-carbon resources directly as far as possible; where they do not participate in the ownership of the concession company, they may require a 'reasonable participation'; a schedule of progressive relinquishing of contract areas should be introduced; and the oil companies shall not have the right to obtain excessively high earnings after taxes.

In 1969 OPEC published the resolutions of its eighteenth conference. One of these directed its Secretary-General to undertake a study with a view to linking posted and tax reference prices to those of the manufactured goods of the major industrialised countries. This marked a definite politicising, and an extension of OPEC's aims and aspirations in two directions: towards control of the activities of foreign oil companies — evident after its 20th Ministerial Conference, according to El Sayed Omar el Badry, its Libyan Secretary-General in 1970; but more than that, a progression into the far wider arena of the developed countries in general. Both trends have continued into the 1970s.

Libyan nationalisation of foreign oil interests in 1970 together with recent Algerian nationalisation of the producing interests of four oil companies led to serious concern in the international oil industry. Iran, Saudi Arabia, Qatar and Venezuela were now running their own marketing companies. In 1970 OPEC demanded 55 per cent as the minimum level of tax on the net income of oil companies operating in OPEC member states — an increase from 50 per cent. It also agreed to end differences in the posted prices of oil in member states, provided that the highest posted price was adopted, after taking into consideration variations among countries.

At OPEC's 1971 meetings it was agreed that its member states had the right to share in 'upstream' (production) and 'downstream' (transport, marketing, processing) operations of the oil companies. A minimum base objective of 20 per cent was initially set; Libya and Algeria wanted a 51 per cent majority share, and Nigeria 37 per cent. The issue of nationalising all unexploited concessions was also raised by Venezuela's action with regard to its oil companies' unexplored concessions. For the first time OPEC supported its demands on Western concession-holding companies with a threat — that of 'unilateral concerted action'.[5]

In 1971 a call by OPEC for higher posted prices of crude oil led to a mammoth increase in oil payments to producers and a rise in the price of oil to the consumers, to compensate for the devaluation of the dollar. This marked the first real impact of OPEC on the rich countries, and the beginning of its being perceived by them as an antagonist. John G. McLean, President and Chief Executive of the Continental Oil Company, urged in his 1971 end-of-year statement that the USA, Western Europe and Japan should join in collective action during 1972 to resist the 'massive' financial demands of major oil producing countries which were now prepared 'to use their power aggressively'.

In 1972 OPEC entered the participation issue, seeking 20 per cent participation in oil companies. Its resolution stated that OPEC, at the request of the member countries concerned, could take 'appropriate action, including sanctions against any company or companies'. The resolution moreover suggested that oil companies might attempt to divide the OPEC ranks by 'submitting to the demands for participation in some member countries and not in others',[6] and indeed this resulted in some differences within OPEC. The companies sought compensation for lost profits on surrendered concessions, and not merely on the net book value of assets. Sheik Ahmed Zaki Yamani of Saudi Arabia had been negotiating on participation for some six months on behalf of the Gulf oil states apart from Iran. The latter decided not to press for participation in concessions held by Western oil companies, and this disrupted an OPEC meeting in Vienna. Moreover the Shah announced that his country had made its separate accommodation with the oil companies.

Towards the end of 1972 an agreement was reached in New York between Sheik Yamani, on behalf of the Gulf states, and the Western oil representatives. This provided the framework within which the Gulf states could eventually achieve a 51 per cent controlling interest in petroleum operations, within an undisclosed period of time. The agreement also formulated the principles upon which producing countries could buy into current operations as well as supply arrangements, to ensure supplies were not disrupted.

OIL PRICE INCREASES

The 11 OPEC countries planned to hold a special Ministerial meeting at Beirut in March 1973 to discuss 'the adverse effects of the dollar devaluation on the purchasing power of the oil revenues'.[7] The meeting was announced after OPEC issued a blunt warning that 'concerted action on the part of the oil importers would have negative effects on the present energy situation'.[8] A three-man team was appointed, consisting of the Libyan Oil Minister Izziddin Al Mabrouk, the Iraqi Oil Minister Sadoon Hammadi, and the Kuwaiti Oil Minister Abdel Rahman Al Attiqi. Its aim was to 'call on the oil companies and start negotiations immediately'[9] to obtain full compensation for the devaluation of the US dollar.

However dispute emerged among the OPEC countries over confrontation with the oil companies, and this involved the cancellation of its conference in May. Saudi Arabia, Abu Dhabi and Iran were unhappy with the direct confrontation sought by the Libyan Oil Minister. The debate concerned the agreed 'Geneva formula' of January 1972 for adjusting posted (or tax reference) prices according to fluctuations in currency exchange rates; Saudi Arabia, Abu Dhabi and Iran had misgivings about abrogating that agreement. Eventually in June 1973 a price formula was negotiated in which OPEC agreed to an increase in posted or tax reference prices of 11.9 per cent.

In July 1973 OPEC issued a policy statement making it clear that oil producers would seek higher prices, and would use oil resources as the primary instrument in accelerating their economic development. In October the Gulf states decided to break off negotiations with the oil companies for a revision of the 1971 Tehran agreement, and to fix their own posted prices unilaterally — an increase of 70 per cent was announced on 16 October; in this action they followed the example of Venezuela, Indonesia and Algeria. However the real shock to the industrialised world came on 23 December 1973 when the Shah of Iran announced that the six main oil producing nations in the Gulf intended to more than double the price of exported oil from January 1974, from about $5.10 to $11.65 a barrel. The Shah was the moving force behind these increases which added over $25,000 million per annum to international oil bills. He had repeatedly pressed for a 'new concept' in fixing oil costs, and argued that the oil price structure should be linked to the cost of other sources of energy. He spoke at a press conference after a meeting attended by Abu Dhabi, Iran, Iraq, Kuwait, Qatar and Saudi Arabia, and with representatives of five other OPEC states — Algeria, Indonesia, Libya, Nigeria and Venezuela — as observers. Some Arab ministers including Sheik Yamani of Saudi Arabia warned the meeting against increases severe enough to cause international economic damage, but the Shah replied that the consumer nations 'will have to realise that the era of their terrific progress and even more terrific income and wealth based on cheap oil is finished'.[10]

At the same time the oil ministers met to consider the oil embargo against countries 'unfriendly' to the Arab cause in the Middle East war, and indicated their intention to supply Britain, France, Japan, Spain and other 'friendly' countries with their 'full oil needs'; by mid 1974 all but a few countries were classified as 'friendly'. A 10 per cent increase in oil production was announced for January 1974, and this reflected, to a certain extent, a concern about causing economic disaster in the developed world that could in turn backfire upon the oil producers themselves.

OECD reaction to the above OPEC measures showed little unanimity. Instead, individual countries like France, Japan and the UK were busy pursuing direct talks with individual Gulf states to ensure their own supplies through trade, arms and technological deals. The US Secretary of State, Dr Kissinger, suggested a forum of major consuming countries to develop common energy approaches. The US attitude was epitomised by a threat of military intervention over the oil price crisis, but this was really meant only as a warning that the Ford Administration's tolerance was limited.[11]

In November 1974 Saudi Arabia, Qatar and Abu Dhabi introduced their own version of a single-price system raising company average costs by 40 cents, and turning their margins on third-party and intra-company trading by 9 cents to 22 cents a barrel. OPEC, in order to achieve the same result, decided (on the basis of a plan submitted by Iran) to combine its single price system for crude against a nine-month freeze on oil prices from January 1975. During 1975 Venezuela took over control of its oil industry, Kuwait took over the remaining 40 per cent interest in the Kuwait oil company held by BP and the Gulf Oil Corporation thus giving its government complete control, while Iraq nationalised all remaining foreign oil units operating in its territory. Similarly in 1976 Saudi Arabia took over the remaining 40 per cent interest in the Arabian American Oil Company.

In December 1976 at its meeting in Qatar a serious difference of opinion among OPEC member states led to a dispute between Saudi Arabia and the others. Sheik Yamani pleaded for a six-month extension of the 18-month price freeze, but this was rejected by all but the United Arab Emirates. Dr Jamshid Amouzegar, the chief Iranian delegate, insisted that most members wanted a 15 per cent increase. A 10 per cent price rise was eventually agreed by the majority for January 1977, with another 5 per cent for July. Saudi Arabia and the United Arab Emirates decided to hold their price increases to 5 per cent, and in addition volunteered to increase their oil output. This division was regarded as ominous for OPEC by some Western newspapers, but Sheik Yamani insisted this was not the case: 'Do not be happy to write off OPEC. It is still a solid organisation.'[12] It was not until mid 1977 that the dispute was resolved. Saudi Arabia then agreed to raise the price of crude to 8 per cent above the 1976 level, thus narrowing the price division in OPEC, and in June the other nine member countries decided to forgo the 5 per cent rise in crude oil prices in order to close the gap. Saudi Arabia nevertheless continued to call for a twelve-month freeze of oil prices during 1978.

This sort of compromise resolution has become the general pattern since then. Saudi Arabia and Iran in particular — the world's largest oil exporters, and the most influential members of OPEC — have attempted not to disrupt economic activity in the West over-drastically, to the point where their own oil revenues have shrunk. This is not unconnected with the fact that OPEC had in 1978 some $40 000 million invested in London and New York banks, and wanted to maintain support for the dollar. At the same time OPEC also seeks to escape dependence on US currency; one way of achieving this would be to index the dollar price of oil against a basket of currencies, but Saudi Arabia does not find this procedure acceptable.

Nevertheless in December 1978 OPEC again raised its oil prices by 14.5 per cent, to take account of the continued depreciation of the dollar, and to compensate its producers for the effects of inflation during the price freeze since July 1977. The unsettled situation in Iran effectively silenced its voice at that time, and cutbacks in its oil production because of strikes, compounded by more recent events, have confirmed this situation.

THIRD WORLD REACTIONS

After the oil price rises of 1 January 1974 the Secretary-General of OPEC, Dr Abdul Rahman Khene, announced that a special bank might be set up to help cushion the ldcs against their effects. When the oil prices were announced several ldcs submitted that they deserved special treatment and should obtain their supplies at a reasonable price. A committee of the OAU decided to seek a meeting with Arab oil producers to discuss the issue, while its Prime Minister, Mr Bhutto, said the sudden rise in prices would increase Pakistan's bill for oil imports to nearly six times its present level, and impede the country's economic progress. A World Bank Paper had shown that ldcs would have to spend about $17 billion (UK) more than they did before, and this would be a 'crushing drain on export earnings'.[13] India made a number of proposals to the OPEC Secretary-General to help its trade over the oil crisis; it calculated that it would have to spend about $2 billion (UK) — about 80 per cent of its expected export earnings — in 1974 to pay for oil imports at the new prices. Its main proposal was for some kind of dual pricing system to give some relief to ldcs. Dr Khene thought this unrealistic in the field of international trade and felt that bilateral trade arrangements might be the best method. But he was of the opinion that some arrangement could be made, and put forward three suggestions: that credit could be arranged from the proposed OPEC bank on easy terms to enable ldcs to pay for their crude imports, that payment for crude imports could be made partly in cash and partly on credit on soft loans, and that there could be some arrangement for bilateral trade whereby developing countries supplied commodities needed by the oil exporting countries.

In March 1974 OPEC announced it would set up a Special Development Fund. Dr Amouzegar, the Iranian Finance Minister, explained that the fund would grant loans to ldcs 'on soft and concessionary terms'. The contributions to the fund were to be voluntary, because some OPEC members like Indonesia had large populations and small oil incomes, so would be unable to contribute as much as other members. Iran envisaged an individual initial contribution of some $120 million, about 1 per cent of oil revenues for 1974. 'We consider that this fund is a lesson for the western and developed world. We asked them to contribute a similar proportion of their wealth to the developing states, but they have not done so. Their output in this sector has, in fact, dropped.'[14] Iran, Venezuela and Algeria firmly sponsored the fund, but Saudi Arabia, Kuwait and the other members did not reach a final decision; the Saudis considered that oil prices were too high, and that OPEC's best contribution to the welfare of the ldcs would be to reduce them. This division meant that OPEC had to attend the Sixth Special Session of the UN without a concrete offer of aid for ldcs.

In 1975 three Arab-sponsored multilateral funds disbursed a total of $268 million; $164 million by the Arab Fund for the Provision of Loans to African Countries, $25 million by the Arab Fund for Economic and Social Development, and $79 million by the Organisation of Arab Petroleum Exporting Countries Special Account to Ease the Financial Burden of the Arab Petroleum Importing Countries. These funds concentrated mainly on African and Arab countries, while the IMF oil facility and the UN Special Fund channelled most OPEC help to India.

In September 1975 Tanzania led an attack on OPEC, after the latest oil price increase. Mr Amir Jamal, its Minister of Commerce and Industries, complained that OPEC seemed to be turning its back on the least developed countries. OPEC agreed to set up a Special Fund in January 1976, in order to provide financial assistance to ldcs other than OPEC members, on concessional terms; these included in particular providing loans to finance balance of payment deficits and development programmes, and to cover contributions to international development agencies whose operations were directed to benefiting developing countries.

OPEC aid to the ldcs remained at some $5.5 billion (UK) from 1975 to 1977, representing over 2 per cent of its GNP, considerably more than that of all developed countries.[15] A 1979 OECD report analysed OPEC aid as follows: OPEC funds are untied, but terms tend to be harder than OECD aid. OPEC concentrates on disbursement to the Arab lands, but this is broadening. Because of inflation its aid, though constant in real terms, has in fact dropped. There is a present tendency towards more project aid and co-financing.

The dilemma facing the oil importing ldcs in their attitude towards OPEC persists to this day, and was clearly evident in 1979 at UNCTAD V at Manila (Chapter 2). Despite massive ldc hardship as a result of OPEC's oil price increases OPEC is still widely perceived by them to be the only force available and exercised by the Third World against the developed countries. And its linkage of oil prices with the cost of imports by the oil producing states has been directly responsible for extending the issue of oil to that of commodities in general in the broader arena of North–South Dialogue which is discussed in Chapter 6.

6 The Conference on International Economic Cooperation (CIEC) 1975-7

NORTH-SOUTH DIALOGUE

The term North-South dialogue has two connotations. In the first place it is now widely used to cover the whole area of negotiations and contact between the developed and underdeveloped world, and has become shorthand for these debates as well as for the issues which have emerged in them. Many of these have already been discussed. In the second place the term refers more specifically to that conference in which lay its direct origins. The CIEC, which began in 1975, rapidly became known as the North-South conference, and concluded in 1977. It is with this connotation and conference that the present chapter is concerned.

HOW THE CIEC CAME ABOUT

In January 1975 the French President, Giscard d'Estaing, made known his intention to invite a dozen countries to a preparatory meeting in Paris to discuss matters relating to oil and the oil price rises. His aim was to 'hold a consumer–producer dialogue'.[1] The original plan called for a tripartite meeting of industrial oil consumers (represented by the USA, Japan and Europe), non-industrial oil consumers (represented by Brazil, India and Zaire) and oil producing countries (represented by Algeria, Nigeria, Saudi Arabia and Iran). However, this breakdown was opposed both by the OPEC countries and the other ldcs as divisive. Hence a consumer–producer dialogue emerged, with the oil producers and other ldcs combined as a single group. Express approval of the proposed conference was given at an OPEC meeting in Algiers, and the French President stressed that this was an initiative undertaken by France and Saudi Arabia and involving 'joint sponsorship'.[2]

The initiative came at a convenient time for OPEC, which was seeking to achieve greater power in international monetary institutions, long-term stability for its favourable balance of payments and cooperation from the developed countries in helping the ldcs. So at its meeting in Algiers in January OPEC called for such a conference and offered various inducements to bring it about. These included an offer to stabilise oil prices for five years starting with a freeze in 1975, an expansion of oil credits which would allow consuming nations to defer their payments, and an acceleration of economic projects that would help consumers to offset their oil debts. To a certain extent this strategy aimed to undermine the position of the US Secretary of State, Dr Kissinger, who was opposed to a producer–consumer meeting until the consumers could unite in their policy towards the OPEC countries.

Most of the developed countries had come to accept, up to a point, the continuation of high oil prices, and had also agreed to establish a $25 billion (UK) 'safety net' fund to protect their economies against the strain of the price rises. This meant that the main preconditions sought by the USA for the conference had been met: that consumers should each develop some sort of energy conservation plan, that a fund should be created to help countries with balance of payment deficits to pay for their oil imports, and that a common floor price for oil imports should be set.

There were divisions within OPEC between countries like Algeria and Iraq which were emphasising OPEC's role as the vanguard of the ldcs, and those like Saudi Arabia, Kuwait and Iran which considered these negotiations to be a way to put relations with the West on a more durable basis. The Shah of Iran informed the French President that it might be possible for oil producers to lower their prices provided this was accompanied by a reduction in the prices of the agricultural and industrial products they needed.[3] Algeria insisted that the conference should discuss not only a broad range of raw materials in addition to oil, but overall relations between rich and poor countries, particularly the industrialisation of the latter. Nevertheless unity in OPEC was still strong, based on its common interest of defending fair prices for oil.

As the conference date approached both groups — 'consumer and producer' — made their ideas and demands known. France backed away from the notion of the 'indexation' of oil prices which had been launched by its President in 1974, as a result of objections by the USA and West Germany. The developed countries instead were now agreed that they should try and convince the ldcs to treat raw materials individually, so that countries like Zambia which were dependent on single products should be dealt with separately at the conference. The US Assistant Secretary of State, Thomas Enders, asserted that Washington aimed to hasten 'the demise' of OPEC.[4] Meanwhile the Third World and OPEC had agreed that the conference should concern itself with the problems of all raw materials and not just oil. The Group of 77 and OPEC also further defined their aims by wanting the talks to be a forum for negotiations on the New International Economic Order.[5]

Two preliminary meetings were held in Paris. At first the working group of five countries could not agree on an agenda but it was eventually agreed to add the subject of raw materials and commodities to the CIEC agenda as well as that of aid to the ldcs. The number of participating countries was increased from 10 to 27: from the developed countries Australia, Canada, the EEC Commission, Japan, Spain, Sweden, Switzerland, USA; from OPEC Algeria, Indonesia, Iran, Iraq, Nigeria, Saudi Arabia, Venezuela; from the ldcs Argentina, Brazil, Cameroon, Egypt, India, Jamacia, Mexico, Pakistan, Peru, Yugoslavia, Zaire, Zambia. The two co-chairmen were to be Allan MacEachen, Canadian Secretary of State for External Affairs, and Manuel Perez-Guerro, Venezuelan Minister of International Affairs. The CIEC conference, at ministerial level, was to take place on 15 December in Paris.

THE PARIS CONFERENCE   DECEMBER 1975

The ministerial conference aim was to begin dialogue between North and South at the highest level. Four commissions were to be set up to deal with the most important problems affecting the relations between oil producers, consumers and the other less developed countries: energy, raw materials, development and finance.[6] The commissions were intended to meet for as long as two years, although first reports were to be provided to another plenary meeting of ministers in six months' time.

Algeria demanded that the mandates for the four special commissions to be set up should be more fully spelled out by the end of

January 1976, and proposed that the two conference chairmen should meet with the commission chairmen at the start of the year in order to work out the guidelines. Both the ldcs and the oil producers supported this proposal; one of its main aims was to ensure that the problem of indexation of oil and raw material prices on industrial imports — one of the Third World's main demands — was included for discussion in one of the commissions.

A confrontation between the USA and some of the oil producers and ldcs developed. Dr Henry Kissinger blamed the world recession and escalating inflation on the massive increase in oil prices over the past two years. The assertion was rejected by the representatives of Iran, Algeria and Iraq, who maintained that the real problems were caused by the industrialised West, which was at this stage coming to terms with the plight of the ldcs only because its own security was threatened. Mr Sadoon Hammadi the Iraqi Foreign Minister, Mr Abdelazis Bouteflika the Algerian Foreign Minister, and Mr Jamshid Amouzegar the Iranian Interior and Oil Minister, demanded the indexation of prices of crude oil and other raw materials to those of imported manufactures and services as a way of remedying the inequalities between the industrialised and underdeveloped countries.

The compromise adopted allowed all members of commissions to raise any relevant subject for discussion, and it was eventually decided to refer the question of defining guidelines for the commissions to another meeting on 26 January. The four commissions each consisted of fifteen members, including ten from the ldcs combined with OPEC, and with two chairmen, one from each side. Saudi Arabia and the USA provided chairmen for the Energy Commission, Japan and Peru for Raw Materials, Algeria and the EEC for Development and Finance. They were to reach decisions for presentation to a ministerial conference in December 1976.

By January 1976 agendas for the commissions were still not agreed. The 19 oil producers and ldcs submitted a list of suggested subjects and the eight dcs reserved the right to submit suggestions once the commissions started work. It was then agreed that they would hold a series of five meetings between February and July.

By July the meetings were again in deadlock over two main issues: debt relief for the poorest countries, and whether and if so how raw material prices should be indexed. This problem was blamed, in a joint statement by the ldcs and oil producers, on the dcs' 'Lack of political will'. The conference co-chairmen were given the task during the summer of trying to get the commissions to resolve the deadlock, and to agree on a work scheme for meetings in September, October and November. The two points at issue were indeed the substance of disagreement at UNCTAD IV at Nairobi in May 1976. Essentially the Third World wanted to commit the developed countries to decide in due course to wipe out the official or government-to-government debt of the poorest countries; they also wanted them to agree to discuss formulae to safeguard their raw material exports.

One of the main difficulties was that the dcs themselves were not united over their strategy towards the Third World. This had been apparent earlier at UNCTAD. The West German Chancellor, Helmut Schmidt, submitted that price increases in the raw material sector would only partially benefit the ldcs, and would in fact be of more benefit to certain rich countries such as the USA, Canada and South Africa; West Germany's insistence was on a free market economy. But unless the developed countries were able to formulate an agreed position, individual approaches would invalidate the concept of North –South dialogue.

By September a compromise had been worked out by the two co-chairmen, and the talks could be resumed. In terms of the compromise the developed countries agreed to discuss ways of relieving debt and preserving the purchasing power of energy and raw material exports. The new agenda was prefaced by a statement which made clear that this did not prejudice the final outcome of the conference, and it implied that the developed countries had not committed themselves in advance to any specific inflation indexation or debt relief.

In November the ldcs increased pressure on the West before OPEC's oil price review of December, by restating their demands for more widescale debt relief, and the oil producers clearly stated that price increases could only be moderated if concessions from the West were forthcoming by mid-December. The eight developed countries were beginning to show signs of agreement on future debt relief arrangements for the most badly affected countries, but not for other ldcs.

Eventually the final North–South ministerial conference was postponed until 1977. A statement issued on behalf of the ldcs blamed the dcs for this decision. Some developed countries claimed they could not 'assume the political positions which will ensure the success of the conference'. This was partly a reference to the USA where the new President had not yet assumed office, and to Japan where a new government was still to be formed. But the decision mainly reflected the gulf between the two sides. The ldcs wanted a moratorium on all repayments of their debts, estimated in 1977 as amounting to $180 000 million (excluding OPEC debts), having doubled over about four years, while the dcs refused to consider this. They were concerned to avoid unilateral default which would give rise to a collapse of banking institutions, and also aimed to isolate debt problems on a case-by-case basis, taking into account the differences between the poorest and the middle-income developing countries.

Although major agreement obviously seemed unlikely to emerge from the CIEC, the rich countries were anxious that its talks should, at least to some degree, be seen to succeed. They wished the CIEC to be seen as part of a continuing process, and its success to be judged by its broader influence. Both sides also felt at this point that the North–South dialogue was not a good forum for discussion between the rich and poor countries. The ldcs, it was reported,[7] believed that it was a mistake to allow the issues to pass beyond UN control, while the dcs felt trapped in a situation where too much depended on the outcome of one set of negotiations.

The final ministerial conference was agreed for 30 May 1977. Shortly before the meeting the ldcs sent an urgent signal to the Western heads of government complaining of lack of interim progress. Developed country proposals, it said, 'fell far short of the magnitude of the problems confronting the developing countries. More enduring and far reaching solutions commensurate with those problems are required to ensure healthy and beneficial effects on the entire world economy.'[8] The 19 insisted that a final agreement must include an integrated programme for commodities, and the establishment of a common fund for the stabilisation of raw material prices. They also called for 'agreements, decisions, commitments and recommendations' on the protection of their export earnings, their debt problems, energy and related international monetary and financial problems, the transfer of resources and technology, access to developed country markets, and aid. Criticism was made of the developed countries' desire to restrict the CIEC to general statements of principle.

THE PARIS CONFERENCE FINAL SESSION MAY 1977

Third World countries, led by Algeria, began the conference by blaming the USA for continually reducing the impact of its 18-month dialogue. There was even some criticism of the setting up of a $1 billion (UK) 'special action fund' by the 8 representatives of the Western industrial countries to be channelled to the poorest countries facing balance of payment problems. This, it was argued, was merely a gesture — 'This programme is supposed to help 800 million people in the poorest countries of the world,' one Third World delegate said, 'that's hardly a dollar each. Meanwhile for nearly two years the rich countries have saved millions of dollars by being able to head off big price rises of raw materials by stringing us along.'[9] Another delegate from the 19 ldcs commented 'The rich countries have at least accepted the principle of interdependence. Unfortunately, this won't be enough to satisfy countries who hoped that the conference would start some sort of economic revolution.'[10]

The conference saw the main ldc demands still being made for the indexing of raw material prices, and a debt moratorium. The USA however made its participation in the billion dollar Action Programme and consideration of a Common Fund to stabilise raw material prices dependent on those Third World demands being dropped. The issue of the Common Fund to finance the buffer stocking of certain key commodities developed into a central one. Originally the fund would be used to buffer-stock 18 commodities, of which UNCTAD designated 10 which deserved priority treatment: tin, copper, rubber, sisal, jute, tea, cocoa, coffee, sugar and cotton.[11] The argument was that both producers and consumers would gain from a stabilisation of prices that a buffer stock could provide, and that a common fund needed less cash than individual commodity agreements because the surplus from the sale on one product could be used to support another. West Germany argued most strongly against the Fund on grounds of free market philosophy, as well as submitting that it would make commodity prices too high; there were also other more detailed arguments that only certain commodities were suited for buffer stocks.

On 31 May the US Secretary of State, Mr Cyrus Vance, in a most significant statement informed the CIEC 'There should be a new international economic system ...' and went on to elaborate upon President Carter's policy intentions towards the ldcs:[12] to join in a one billion dollar international fund for agricultural development; to argue for an increase in US aid; to support an increase in World Bank capital; to support the EEC's proposed special action programme to help ldcs — the EEC proposed that the USA and itself would contribute $375 billion (UK); the establishment of aid for specific programmes to alleviate absolute poverty on a global basis; a readiness to participate in action to moderate fluctuations in commodity prices, supplies and earnings, including a Common Fund.

Nevertheless by the end of the CIEC on 2 June 1977, despite some agreement,[13] after two days of bargaining most of the key issues had not been resolved. The conference failed to agree on a plan to deal with the debts of the ldcs, apart from those of the very poor; its communiqué reported 'The participants could not reach an agreement on the various aspects of external indebtedness'.[14] Neither would the developed countries as a group commit themselves to devote as much as 0.7 per cent of their GNPs to development aid, although Sweden, Norway and the Netherlands in fact exceeded that figure.[15] The only agreement on the Common Fund was a general statement supporting it, with the details being left to future negotiations in UNCTAD. A final statement[16] released on 3 June noted that the Third World, while recognising that some progress had been made, regretted that structural change in the international economic system had not been agreed.

Conclusion

It is clear to everyone that so far the North–South dialogue has failed, and the New International Economic Order is still a dream. The differences between the developed and underdeveloped ends of the spectrum remain; the gap is widening, and polarisation is increasing.

The development of Third World political organisation outlined in this book is a frustrating one; a record of halting progress and count-less setbacks, of differences and divisions not only between the dcs and the ldcs but within the ranks of the ldcs themselves. But it is a con-tinuing process, a persistent one, and one which must proceed and may indeed prevail.

Third World progress obviously depends both upon its own efforts and upon what the developed world does to help; one is of no avail without the other. But it is clear that its advances have been most evident when it has itself achieved success, when it is united in its goals and in the tactics for achieving them; and when it is able to exercise power, as OPEC has done. Then it can no longer be ignored.

And one lesson has not been lost on its people: that success, if there is to be success, — and what else can be envisaged in the face of so much human misery — will be achieved through political organisa-tion.

Appendix

Date Chart of Main Events Affecting the Third World 1944–80
Most important events italicised

DATE Year	Day	Month	PLACE	EVENTS IN CHRONOLOGICAL ORDER	ORGANISATION	MAIN CONTENT/RESULT/ COMMENT
1944	1–22	7	Bretton Woods, USA	International Monetary and Financial Conference of the United and Associated Nations agreed to establish the IMF and IBRD	IMF/IBRD	Establishment of the IMF and IBRD (inaugural meeting of Boards of Governors 8.3.1946, Savannah, USA)
1944			Brazzaville, Congo	Brazzaville Conference		Self-government in the French colonies rejected
1945	26	6	San Francisco, USA	San Francisco Conference and UN Charter Preamble signed	UN	Establishment of the UN
1946				De Gaulle first expressed the idea of a 'Third Force' in world affairs, consisting of African and Asian countries		The 'Third Force' later became neutralism and the Afro-Asian bloc
1947		3		Interim Coordinating Committee of International Commodity Arrangements established	ECOSOC	Prepared for ECOSOC the 'Review of International Commodity Problems'
1947			Harvard, USA	Speech by Secretary of State Marshall proposing European Recovery Programme (ERP, Marshall Plan)	MARSHALL PLAN	Europe rebuilt after the Second World War
1947	30	10	Geneva, Switzerland	The General Agreement on Trade and Tariffs (GATT) signed by 32 countries	GATT	To regulate trade and negotiate tariff reductions. At first it was temporary until the Havana Charter (Már 1948, signed by 53 countries) was operating with the International Trade Organisation (ITO), but became permanent. N.B. MFN clause of Article 1: relief from tariff charges must be granted to all members. Major concessions achieved on free trade by the USA lead in this meeting

Date Chart of Main Events Affecting the Third World 1944–80
Most important events italicised

DATE Year	Day	Month	PLACE	EVENTS IN CHRONOLOGICAL ORDER	ORGANISATION	MAIN CONTENT/RESULT/ COMMENT
1947 (to Mar 1948)	11		Cuba	International Conference on Trade and Employment. Havana Charter signed Mar 1948		To establish an International Trade Organisation. Initially proposed by UK and USA in 1945 as part of Bretton Woods system leading to the elimination of trade restrictions and tariff barriers. Contained many escape clauses. GATT led to its demise
1947			Delhi, India	All-Asian Conference		
1948			Bogota, Colombia	Bogota Conference. Organisation of American States founded	OAS	OAS established
1948			South Africa	National Party Government under Dr Malan in power. 'Apartheid Manifesto'		The beginning of the Apartheid policy
1949	1			COMECON established	COMECON	
1949			Annecy, France	GATT Conference	GATT	Protectionism beginning to reassert itself particularly in USA. No agreement between USA and UK and Commonwealth
1950			Torquay, UK	GATT Conference		
1950	8			ECOSOC authorised the Secretary General to convene intergovernmental conferences on specific commodity problems	ECOSOC	Commodities
1951	8			ECOSOC asked IBRD to study setting up an International Finance Corporation as a subsidiary organisation of the Bank	ECOSOC/IBRD	To provide an additional flow of capital from private sources which was internationally controlled. In April 1952 the President of the IBRD submitted a report on the proposal for an IFC in favour of the ldcs, and this was established in 1956 as a World Bank affiliate

Date Chart of Main Events Affecting the Third World 1944–80
Most important events italicised

DATE Year	Day	Month	PLACE	EVENTS IN CHRONOLOGICAL ORDER	ORGANISATION	MAIN CONTENT/RESULT/ COMMENT
1951				Colombo Plan for Cooperative Economic Development in South and S.E. Asia in operation	COLOMBO PLAN	21 nations included. Bilateral negotiations, although a system of cooperation. The idea began in meeting of Commonwealth Foreign Ministers in 1950
1951	21	12		Commonwealth Sugar Agreement	COMMON-WEALTH	8-year agreement embodying a contract by the exporting parties to supply (and by the UK Ministry of Agriculture to buy) agreed quantities of sugar each year at fixed prices
1954	1			International Sugar Agreement	UN	Commodities
1954	28	(to 2 May)		First meeting of Colombo powers (India, Pakistan, Burma, Ceylon, Indonesia)	NON-ALIGNED	India proposed convening Afro-Asian Conference in 1954
1954			Bogor, Indonesia	Meeting of Colombo powers to decide on Afro-Asian Conference	NON-ALIGNED	Bangkok SEATO Conference announced a week before meeting, possibly to distract diplomatic interest from the Afro-Asian Conference (SEATO established Sep 1954)

Date Chart of Main Events Affecting the Third World 1944–80
Most important events italicised

DATE Year	Day	Month	PLACE	EVENTS IN CHRONOLOGICAL ORDER	ORGANISATION	MAIN CONTENT/RESULT/ COMMENT
1954	30	4		Permanent Advisory Commission of International Commodity Trade established (ECOSOC Res. 512, 17th Session)	ECOSOC	To examine measures designed to avoid excessive fluctuation in the prices and volume of trade in primary Commodities, including measures aiming at the maintenance of a just and equitable relationship between the prices of primary commodities and those of manufactured goods in international trade. The Commission was revised in GATT's Ninth Session in 1954 to reduce conflict between economic development and other countries' short-term interests
1954			Rome, Italy	World Population Conference	UN	Population
1954 (to 7 Mar 1955)	28	10	Geneva, Switzerland	GATT Review Conference, Ninth Session	GATT	Main principles reaffirmed, and parts of GATT code strengthened. Proposal for Organisation for Trade Cooperation to administer GATT
1955			Bandung, Indonesia	*Asian-African Conference. Bandung Declaration*	*NON-ALIGNED AND OTHERS*	Reaffirmed the 'Five Principles' first formulated by China and India in 1954: respect for territorial sovereignty, non-interference in the internal affairs of other countries, equality and mutual benefit, non-aggression, peaceful coexistence. The policy of non-alignment was developed. The conference marked the emergence of China as a political force in Asia

Date Chart of Main Events Affecting the Third World 1944–80
Most important events italicised

DATE Year	Day	Month	PLACE	EVENTS IN CHRONOLOGICAL ORDER	ORGANISATION	MAIN CONTENT/RESULT/COMMENT
1956				International Wheat Agreement	UN	Commodities
1956	1	7		International Tin Agreement	UN	Commodities
1957			Cairo, Egypt	Afro-Asian Solidarity Conference		
1957			Rome, Italy	Treaty of Rome which led to establishment of the EEC	EEC	Of 6 European countries at first. Part IV was concerned with the 'Association of Overseas Countries and Territories'
1958			Geneva, Switzerland	UN Conference on Lead and Zinc	UN	Commodities
1958				Haberler Report to GATT	GATT	Highlighted the special problems of ldcs and seemed to presage the granting of a higher priority to these in GATT
1958			Montreal, Canada	Commonwealth Economic Conference	COMMON-WEALTH	The subject of commodity stabilisation was raised. For the first time the new Afro-Asian members balanced the Western ones in numbers
1959	30	6		International Agreement on Olive Oil	UN	Commodities
1959		12		International Development Bank	UN	Created to extend soft loans to countries, in special circumstances
1959				International Wheat Agreement	UN	Commodities
1960 *(to Jan 1965)*	*1*			*Over 25 African countries became independent during this period*		Decolonisation in Africa
1960				OPEC's first conference	OPEC	OPEC established to strengthen petroleum producers' power

Date Chart of Main Events Affecting the Third World 1944–80
Most important events italicised

DATE Year	Day	Month	PLACE	EVENTS IN CHRONOLOGICAL ORDER	ORGANISATION	MAIN CONTENT/RESULT/COMMENT
1960				UN adopted a target for the amount of capital transferred by developed countries to ldcs: 1% of combined national incomes of dcs	UN	Development aid target first accepted
1960				UN Capital Development Fund	UN – GENERAL ASSEMBLY	Development finance
1960				ECOSOC established a standing Committee for Industrial Development	ECOSOC	Industrial development increasingly recognised as important. In Nov 1961 this committee produced a 'Declaration on the Promotion of the trade of Ldcs'
1960 (to 1962)			Geneva, Switzerland	GATT conference	GATT	Trade and tariff discussions
1961		8		Alliance for Progress		20 member states of OAS met to design a long-term programme of regional development for South America. Produced Charter of Punta del Este. Launched by the Kennedy Administration
1961	30	9		OECD formally established	OECD	OECD in existence
1961	19	12		First UN Development Decade	UN	10-year development plan. Goal of 5% annual growth rate in total domestic product
1961			*Belgrade, Yugoslavia*	*First summit meeting of non-aligned countries (25 members)*	NON-ALIGNED	Principles of non-alignment established. Attended by 24 Afro-Asian states and Cuba. Dominated by Nehru, Nasser, Nkrumah, Sukarno, Tito. Anti Cold War

Date Chart of Main Events Affecting the Third World 1944–80
Most important events italicised

DATE Year	Day	Month	PLACE	EVENTS IN CHRONOLOGICAL ORDER	ORGANISATION	MAIN CONTENT/RESULT/ COMMENTS
1961	19	12		Centre for Industrialisation established		Industrial development
1961 (to 1962)				Dillon Round of Tariff Negotiations	GATT	Carried out partly on a commodity by commodity basis, and partly on an 'across the board' basis
1962	7	3	USA	Second International Tin Agreement	UN	Commodities
1962				US Trade Expansion Act		Considerably increased the authority of the President to negotiate cuts in the US tariff
1962	1	6		Commissioner for Industrial Development appointed	UN	Development-industrial
1962	9–18	7	Cairo, Egypt	Cairo Conference and Cairo Declaration on Problems of Developing Countries	UN	Signed by 36 ldcs. Declaration: ldcs should cooperate to strengthen UN economic and social activity
1962	1	8		International Wheat Agreement	UN	Commodities
1962				*ECOSOC session resolved to convene UNCTAD* (3 years)	*ECOSOC/ UNCTAD*	To mould international trade into a form more helpful to the ldcs
1963	1	1		World Food Programme	UN	Three year experiment at first
1963	4–20	2		UN Conference on the Application of Science and Technology for the Less Developed Areas (UNCSAT)	UN	
1963	5		Addis Ababa, Ethiopia	Conference of Heads of non-white African States (not Togo and Morocco)	OAU	Draft Charter of the OAU on the confederate pattern adopted. Liberation of colonies a major theme

Date Chart of Main Events Affecting the Third World 1944–80
Most important events italicised

DATE Year	Day	Month	PLACE	EVENTS IN CHRONOLOGICAL ORDER	ORGANISATION	MAIN CONTENT/RESULT/COMMENTS
1963	20	7	Yaounde, Cameroon	First Yaounde Convention. In operation from 1 June 1964		Convention of Association between 6 EEC states and 18 African states (unofficially signed on 20 Dec 1962). Provided for special and reverse preferences. This gave rise to criticism by the Group of 77
1963	8		Dakar, Senegal	First meeting of OAU Council of Ministers	OAU	Union Africaine et Malgache (UAM) and Casablanca Bloc disbanded because of their political nature
1963	27	12		International Coffee Agreement	UN	Commodities
1964 (to June 1977)				Kennedy Round (6th Conference)	GATT	Hopes of gains for ldcs during this round, so the 'moderate' group in UNCTAD gave its support
1964				International Trade Centre established within GATT	GATT	To give trade information and advice to ldcs
1964	2			*Joint Declaration of the 77 Developing Countries (currently over 100 members)*	*GROUP OF 77*	Group of 77 established to define a joint ldc position with regard to UNCTAD
1964			*Geneva, Switzerland*	*UNCTAD 1*	*UNCTAD*	The conference put forward strong criticisms of the dcs and the international trade system, and had these accepted by most dcs except the USA
1964			*Cairo, Egypt*	*Second summit meeting of non-aligned countries (47 members)*	*NON-ALIGNED*	'Programme for Peace' adopted. Support given to Palestinians for first time. Concentration on economic development

Date Chart of Main Events Affecting the Third World 1944–80
Most important events italicised

DATE Year	Day	Month	PLACE	EVENTS IN CHRONOLOGICAL ORDER	ORGANISATION	MAIN CONTENT/RESULT/ COMMENTS
1965				ECOSOC and General Assembly adopted resolutions demanding further action with regard to the Development Decade	ECOSOC	
1965	9		Belgrade, Yugoslavia	World Population Conference	UN	Western concern with the population explosion. These views criticised by the Communist countries
1965				*Part IV added to GATT*	*GATT*	GSPs introduced, i.e. no 'reciprocity' necessary from ldcs to dcs in tariffs. (Suggestion which gave rise to UNCTAD's demands first made within GATT in 1961 by India)
1965	10		Accra, Ghana	OAU Heads of State meeting	OAU	Debate on giving more power to the OAU (sponsored by Nkrumah)
1965				First and Second sessions of the Trade and Development Board	UNCTAD	Trade and Development Board meets annually. It has 6 main Committees
1966	1	1		UNDP formed from EPTA (Expanded Programme of Technical Assistance) and the UN Special Fund	UNDP	
1966		1	Havana, Cuba	First Afro-Asian-Latin American People's Solidarity Conference (OSPAAAL)	NON-ALIGNED AND OTHERS	First Conference after Bandung (attempts to hold a 'Second Bandung' in 1965 failed). Second OSPAAAL in 1968 did not take place because of 1967 Middle East War
1966			Rome, Italy	World Land Reform Conference	UN/FAO/ILO	Theme: land reform necessary for development

Date Chart of Main Events Affecting the Third World 1944–80
Most important events italicised

DATE Year	Day	Month	PLACE	EVENTS IN CHRONOLOGICAL ORDER	ORGANISATION	MAIN CONTENT/RESULT/ COMMENTS
1966	6		Seoul, South Korea	Asian Foreign Ministers Conference, and Asian and Pacific Council established (ASPAC)	ASPAC	Objective: to maintain consultations on regional problems and promote regional cooperation and stability. India and Ceylon did not attend. Initiative for conference taken in Bangkok
1966				Third International Tin Agreement	UNCTAD	Commodities
1966	30	6		Third Session of Trade and Development Board	UNCTAD	
1966				UN Capital Development Fund	UN GENERAL ASSEMBLY	To help ldcs in economic development by supplementing their existing sources of capital assistance by means of grants and loans. N.B. long-term loans at low or no interest
1966			HQ in Manila, Philippines	Asian Development Bank begins operations		Set up to develop the area's economy through international cooperation
1967	1	1	HQ in Vienna, Austria	UNIDO established	UNIDO	To promote and accelerate the industrial development of ldcs and to coordinate UN activities in this area
1967			*Algiers, Algeria*	*Group of 77 Ministerial Meeting (86 members) Charter of Algiers signed*	*GROUP OF 77*	In preparation for UNCTAD II. Theme: National sovereignty and natural resources
1967				ASEAN established	ASEAN	First Ministerial Conference in Djakarta in Aug 1968 agreed to set up permanent bodies to cooperate in certain areas
1968				UNCTAD becomes a participatory agency in UNDP	UNCTAD	

Date Chart of Main Events Affecting the Third World 1944–80
Most important events italicised

DATE Year	Day	Month	PLACE	EVENTS IN CHRONOLOGICAL ORDER	ORGANISATION	MAIN CONTENT/RESULT/ COMMENTS
1968		*2*	*Delhi, India*	*UNCTAD II*	*UNCTAD*	Resolution calling for the 'early establishment of a mutually acceptable system of generalised non-reciprocal and non-discriminating preferences which would be beneficial to the developing countries' (GSPs). This would contain specific measures for the least advanced countries
1968				Sugar Agreement	UNCTAD	
1969		4	Lusaka, Zambia	Lusaka Manifesto on Southern Africa		Issued after a series of meetings of 14 African states, and adopted by the Sixth OAU Assembly of Heads of State and Government in Sep 1969. A commitment to bring about majority rule in Africa by peaceful means at first, but by violence as a last resort
1969		5		Agreement of Cartagena to set up Andean Common Market	ANCOM	Adean Common Market
1969	29	7	Yaounde, Cameroon	Second Yaounde Convention signed (in operation on 1 June 1971)		The Common External Tariff diminished Yaounde II's discriminatory effects on non-associated ldcs. Production aids to permit marketing at world prices were dropped from the agreement

Date Chart of Main Events Affecting the Third World 1944–80
Most important events italicised

DATE Year	Day	Month	PLACE	EVENTS IN CHRONOLOGICAL ORDER	ORGANISATION	MAIN CONTENT/RESULT/COMMENTS
1969				Pearson Report published	IBRD	'Partners in Development' prepared for the World Bank by the Commission on International Development, chaired by Lester B. Pearson. Dealt with the problems and policies of aid, and concluded optimistically. It considered aid a moral obligation
1969				Jackson Report published	UNDP	'A study of the capacity of the UN development system' (UNDO/5), directed by Sir Robert Jackson. It dealt with the effectiveness of multilateral aid, and was critical of it
1969	10		Rabat, Morocco	UNIDO promotion meeting for all African countries	UNIDO	
1970			Lusaka, Zambia	*Third non-aligned countries Summit of Heads of State (53 members)*	*NON-ALIGNED*	Self-reliance was the theme. The non-aligned countries considered controlling foreign direct investment for the first time
1970	1	1		Second Development Decade	UN	10-year development plan
1971	1	1		Group of 24 set up by the Group of 77	GROUP OF 77/ GROUP OF 24	To coordinate matters related to the international monetary system

Appendix

Date Chart of Main Events Affecting the Third World 1944–80
Most important events italicised

DATE Year	Day	Month	PLACE	EVENTS IN CHRONOLOGICAL ORDER	ORGANISATION	MAIN CONTENT/RESULT/ COMMENTS
1971	26	6		GATT meeting	GATT	In accord with the broad purposes of Part IV GATT voted 'to authorise the introduction by developed member countries of generalised, non-discriminatory preferential tariff treatment for products originating in developing countries' (for 10 years — GSPs)
1971	10		Lima, Peru	*Group of 77 Ministerial meeting (95 members)*	*GROUP OF 77*	In preparation for UNCTAD III. Theme: national sovereignty over natural resources
1971	18	12	Washington, USA	Washington Monetary Agreement	GROUP OF TEN	To establish a new set of commodity arrangements after President Nixon had suspended the convertibility of the dollar into gold (August)
1972			Santiago, Chile	*UNCTAD III*	*UNCTAD*	Charter of the economic rights and duties of states adopted
1972			USA	US Tariff Commission produced report on the role of multinational enterprises in global economics		The report stated that 'governments have absolutely no control' and even with no 'destructive and predatory motives' the multinationals can cause monetary crises by moving their money between countries

Date Chart of Main Events Affecting the Third World 1944–80
Most important events italicised

DATE Year	Day	Month	EVENTS IN CHRONOLOGICAL ORDER	PLACE	ORGANISATION	MAIN CONTENT/RESULT/COMMENTS
1972			Third Conference of Ministers of the Non-aligned Movement	Georgetown, Guyana	NON-ALIGNED	'Action Programme for Economic Cooperation' agreed. Decided to establish Committee of Experts of the Non-aligned Countries on private Foreign Investment. Conference influenced by Chinese. Similar to ideas in UNCTAD III
1972	26	7	Committee on the Reform of the International Monetary System and Related Issues (Committee of 20) established by Board of Governors of the IMF		COMMITTEE OF 20/IMF	To advise IMF/Board of Governors, and to prepare proposals for comprehensive reform. Last meeting (6th) held June 1974
1972		7	ECOSOC resolution asking Secretary-General to appoint Group of Eminent Persons to Study Transnational Enterprises		ECOSOC/GROUP OF EMINENT PERSONS	In 1974 a report was published (The Impact of Multinational Corporations on Development and International Relations, ST/ECA/6) recommending that a separate commission on multinational corporations should be established as a subsidiary body of ECOSOC; the Secretary-General endorsed the report. This followed a report in 1973 by the UN Dept of Economic and Social Affairs (ST/ECA/190)
1972	10	10	Last meeting under the Yaounde Agreement	Luxembourg	YAOUNDE	

Date Chart of Main Events Affecting the Third World 1944–80
Most important events italicised

DATE Year	Day	Month	PLACE	EVENTS IN CHRONOLOGICAL ORDER	ORGANISATION	MAIN CONTENT/RESULT/ COMMENTS
1973	1	1		UK, Ireland and Denmark join the EEC	EEC	
1973	30	6		International Cocoa Agreement	UNCTAD	Commodities
1973		*9*	*Algiers, Algeria*	*Fourth Summit of the Non-aligned Countries (75 members)*	*NON-ALIGNED*	Called for UN 6th Special Session on development and cooperation. Framework of the NIEO outlined for the first time, emphasising collective self-reliance, national sovereignty over natural resources, national control over private foreign investment in ldcs. Called for ldc meeting to decide strategy concerning primary products
1973		9	Santiago, Chile	Committee of Experts of Non-aligned Countries on Private Foreign Investment	NON-ALIGNED	Santiago Declaration of results to be submitted to 4th Non-aligned Summit in Algiers
1973		10	Middle East	Oil embargo imposed and oil prices raised during Arab-Israeli War	OPEC	Oil prices quadrupled. Posted prices: 1. 6. 1973: $ 2.898 b/d 16. 10. 1973: $ 5.119 b/d 1. 1. 1974: $11.651 b/d
1974	17	1	Rome, Italy	Committee of 20 decided to adopt evolutionary approach to reform	COMMITTEE OF 20	'Outline of Reform' issued and work concluded 14 June 1974

Date Chart of Main Events Affecting the Third World 1944–80
Most important events italicised

DATE Year	Day	Month	PLACE	EVENTS IN CHRONOLOGICAL ORDER	ORGANISATION	MAIN CONTENT/RESULT/COMMENTS
1974	18–21	3	Maryland, USA	Conference on World Development. Belmont Statement	OVERSEAS DEVELOPMENT COUNCIL/ CHARLES F. KETTERING FOUNDATION	Statement released 2 months before the 6th Special Session of the UN General Assembly. Evidence of support at the private level in the developed countries of the NIEO. Stressed self-reliance and international reform
1974	*9 (to 2 May)*	*4*	*New York, USA*	*6th Special Session of the UN General Assembly*	*UN GENERAL ASSEMBLY*	Called for by the Non-aligned President. Declaration and Programme for Action on NIEO adopted (General Assembly resolution 3201 S-VI, 3202 S-VI). Raw materials and development the main themes, and a special general programme to help the MSA countries adopted
1974		4		Gamani Corea of Sri Lanka became Secretary-General of UNCTAD	UNCTAD	
1974		7		Kingston Memorandum on Industrial Cooperation	ACP	ACP representatives presented policies. Title 3 of the Lomé Convention based on these
1974	19–30	8	Bucharest, Rumania	UN World Population Conference	UN	World Population Plan of Action

Appendix

Date Chart of Main Events Affecting the Third World 1944–80
Most important events italicised

DATE Year	Day	Month	PLACE	EVENTS IN CHRONOLOGICAL ORDER	ORGANISATION	MAIN CONTENT/RESULT/ COMMENTS
1974	8	10	Cocoyoc, Mexico	International symposium on 'Patterns of Resource Use, Environment and Development Strategies'. COCOYOC Declaration	UNEP/UNCTAD	Declaration endorsed the 'very preliminary steps' taken by the 6th Special Session and encouraged the early adoption of the Charter of Economic Rights and Duties of States. Important personal statements by dc and ldc experts
1974	5–16	11	Rome, Italy	World Food Conference	UN	In response to food crisis. Led to various resolutions e.g. the setting up of the World Food Concil
1974	12	12		*29th UN Session adopted Charter of Economic Rights and Duties of States*	UN	Under negotiation in UNCTAD since 1972 (General Assembly resolution 3281 XXIX). Concerned with multinational enterprise as well as other reforms
1974	17	12		UN General Assembly adopted a resolution on reform of the International Monetary System	UN GENERAL ASSEMBLY	
1975	1			OECD Committee on International Investment and Multinational Enterprises established	OECD	Multinationals
1975	5–10	1	Karachi, Pakistan	Third World Forum inaugural meeting	THIRD WORLD	NIEO discussed. Supported Santiago Declaration. Main function to provide an intellectual platform and support for change in development policies

Date Chart of Main Events Affecting the Third World 1944–80
Most important events italicised

DATE Year	Day	Month	PLACE	EVENTS IN CHRONOLOGICAL ORDER	ORGANISATION	MAIN CONTENT/RESULT/COMMENTS
1975	4–8	2	Dakar, Senegal	Conference of Developing Countries on raw materials	UN	Theme: raw materials. Set basis for ldc coordination. Call for a FAO-UNCTAD ministerial conference to deal with shortages of food and to maintain stable prices. (UN Document E/AC 62/6)
1975	28	2	Lomé, Togo	Lomé Convention	LOMÉ	New agreement between EEC and ACP countries. 'Stabex' introduced. Reverse preferences ended
1975	27	3	Lima, Peru	Second General Conference of UNIDO. Lima Declaration (UN document ID/Conf 3/31)	UNIDO	UNIDO transformed into a specialised agency. A change to the multisectoral approach to industrial development. The indigenous development of science and technology urged. Advocated a redeployment of world industrial capacity to increase the ldc share. Widened scope of international co-operation.
1975	19 (to 2 July)	6	Mexico	World Conference of International Women's Year	UN	Declaration of Mexico. Three aims adopted: equality, development, peace

Date Chart of Main Events Affecting the Third World 1944–80
Most important events italicised

DATE Year	Day	Month	PLACE	EVENTS IN CHRONOLOGICAL ORDER	ORGANISATION	MAIN CONTENT/RESULT/COMMENTS
1975	25–30	8	Lima, Peru	Non-aligned Foreign Ministers' Conference (just before UN 7th Special Session)	NON-ALIGNED	Solidarity Fund for Economic and Social Development established. Special Fund for the Financing of Buffer Stocks of Raw Materials and Primary Products exported by Developing Countries established. Adopted by UN (UN document A/10217)
1975				*UN 7th Special Session*	*UN GENERAL ASSEMBLY*	Theme: Development and International Economic Cooperation. Consensus resolution on 16 Sep. Code of conduct for multinationals suggested
1975 (to 2 June 1977)	12		Paris, France	CIEC Conference (North–South Dialogue)	CIEC	High-level meeting to discuss development between ldcs, oil producers and dcs. Results inconclusive
1976	7	1		Communiqué of Intergovernmental Group of 24	GROUP OF 24	International monetary affairs
1976	*1*		*Manila, Philippines*	*Group of 77 Ministerial Meeting (112 members) Declaration of Manila*	*GROUP OF 77*	To prepare for UNCTAD IV. Declaration of Manila signed. The Group of 77's Economic Action Programme was accepted, and a decision to convene an economic conference in 1977 was taken
1976	5		*Nairobi, Kenya*	*UNCTAD IV*	*UNCTAD*	Integrated Programme for commodities adopted. Ldc debt problems discussed
1976	31 (to 11 June)	5	Vancouver, Canada	HABITAT: UN conference on human settlements	UN	6th in a series of conferences. Recommended an international secretariat for human settlements

Date Chart of Main Events Affecting the Third World 1944–80
Most important events italicised

DATE Year	Day	Month	PLACE	EVENTS IN CHRONOLOGICAL ORDER	ORGANISATION	MAIN CONTENT/RESULT/ COMMENT
1976		6		ILO World Employment Conference	ILO	Programme of Action adopted which endorsed the 'basic needs' approach to development
1976	9–19	8	Colombo, Sri Lanka	*Fifth Summit of the Non-aligned Countries (86 members)*	*NON-ALIGNED*	Action Programme for Economic Co-operation agreed. Economic warning to the West
1976		9	Mexico	*Group of 77 Conference on Economic Cooperation in Development Countries*	*GROUP OF 77*	Decision taken to hold annual ministerial meetings instead of simply preparing for UNCTAD. Support for Integrated Programme for Commodities
1977		3	*Geneva, Switzerland*	*1st Negotiating Conference on a Common Fund*	*UNCTAD*	Broke down but agreed to meet again soon
1977	29 (to 9 Sep)	8		UN Conference on Desertification	UN	From General Assembly resolution in 1974, following concern about desertification. Led to Plan of Action to combat desertification
1977	7	11	*Geneva, Switzerland*	*2nd UNCTAD Negotiating Conference on a Common Fund*	*UNCTAD*	Attended by 104 countries. Common Fund and Integrated Programme for Commodities generally seen as an important part of the NIEO by the ldcs
1978		3	Geneva, Switzerland	Trade and Development Board met to discuss debt	UNCTAD	Third World debt discussed. Efforts to get dcs to write off 'official development assistance' debts

Date Chart of Main Events Affecting the Third World 1944–80
Most important events italicised

| DATE | | PLACE | EVENTS IN CHRONOLOGICAL ORDER | ORGANISATION | MAIN CONTENT/RESULT/ COMMENTS |
Year	Day Month				
1979	7 5 (to 3 June)	*Manila, Philippines*	*UNCTAD V (pre-conference of senior officials, 3–4 May)*	*UNCTAD*	$87m pledged to the 'second window' (commodity development facility) of the Common Fund for Commodities. Main issues: the NIEO, protectionism. No agreement
1979	12–20 7	Rome, Italy	FAO World Conference on Agrarian Reform and Rural Development	FAO	Declaration of Principles and Programme of Action
1979	9	*Havana, Cuba*	*Sixth Summit of the Non-aligned Countries*	*NON-ALIGNED*	Political disputes dominated discussion. Little achieved
1980	3	*London, UK*	*The Brandt Report published (North–South: A Programme for Survival)*	*Independent Commission on International Development Issues* Willy Brandt (West Germany, Head of Commission)	Theme: interdependence; economic growth in one country depends on growth elsewhere. The North depends on developing the South for its continuing prosperity and the South depends on the North for its development. Main recommendations: massive transfer of resources from dcs to ldcs (concept of international tax introduced); restructuring of international relations, particularly with regard to commodities and industrialisation; a World Development Fund should be created; world energy strategy; monetary reform; food programme; institutional reform (e.g. of World Bank); action programme for the poorest.

Notes

CHAPTER 1: UNCTAD I

1. Quoted in D. Cordovez, 'The making of UNCTAD', *Journal of World Trade Law,* Vol. 1, No. 3 (1967).
2. Ibid.
3. Official records of the Economic and Social Council: 34th session, 1236th meeting, p. 209, para 17, ECOSOC res 917 (XXXIV) of 3 VIII (1962).
4. (i) The Havana Charter with the concept of an International Trade Organisation (ITO) signed by 53 countries in March 1948. (ii) 30/10/1947 GATT signed, and in 1954 the Organisation for Trade Cooperation (OTC) was agreed to administer GATT. (iii) The Haberler Report was presented to GATT 1958. (iv) 1957 The Treaty of Rome led to the establishment of the EEC. (v) 1961–2 The Dillon Round of tariff negotiations. (vi) November 1961 Declaration on Promotion of Trade of Ldcs agreed. (vii) May 1963 GATT ministerial meeting accepted the Action Programme. (viii) 1964–7 the Kennedy Round.
5. International Trade, GATT Secretariat (1954) p. 128.
6. 'Commodity and Trade Problems of Developing Countries: institutional arrangements', Report of a Group of Experts appointed under Economic and Social Council resolution 919 (xxxiv) Document E/3756 (1963).
7. The Haberler Report (Trends in International Trade: a report by a Panel of Experts, GATT, Sales No. GATT/1950–3, Oct 1958) was submitted to GATT; it highlighted the special problems of ldcs and seemed to presage the granting of a higher priority to them.
8. Report of the OECD Group (OECD doc. TC(64)), 4 February 1964, p. 28. Quoted in B. Gosovic, *UNCTAD: Conflict and Compromise,* Sijthoff, Leiden (1972) p. 23.
9. Statement by the representative of India, Sir Raglavan Pillai, at the ninth session of the Contracting Parties to GATT. Quoted in D. Cordovez, op.cit., p. 268.
10. *Sunday Telegraph,* 24.9.61.
11. *Dawn,* 30.1.63.
12. E.g. Indonesia, *Dawn,* 19.4.64.
13. Memorandum of the Brazilian Delegation to the 1962 General Assembly on the Institutional Framework for the Expansion of International Trade, A/C2/214. Quoted in D. Cordovez, op.cit.
14. UN General Assembly Resolution 1027 (XI). Quoted in F. Parkinson, 'Soviet aid to underdeveloped countries', *The Yearbook of World Affairs,* Vol. 11 (1957).
15. *New York Times,* 20.6.64.
16. Noted by S. Strange, 'The Commonwealth and the Sterling Area'. *The Yearbook of World Affairs,* Vol. 13 (1959).

17. *Dawn,* 21.3.64.
18. B. Gosovic, op.cit.
19. Stressed in *Dawn,* 19.6.64.
20. Proceedings, Vol. 1, pp. 67–8.
21. ODI Briefing paper No. 3 (1978).
22. Quoted in B. Gosovic, op.cit., p. 291.
23. Ibid.

CHAPTER 2:   UNCTAD II, III, IV, V

1. D. Cordovez, 'Unctad and development policy'. In 'Confrontation to strategy', *Journal of World Trade Law* (1972) p. 75.
2. Ibid., p. 76.
3. *Hindu,* 8.3.1968.
4. *Guardian,* 14.2.1968.
5. *International Herald Tribune,* 8.2.1968.
6. *Financial Times,* 29.3.1968.
7. *Observer,* Foreign News Service, 2.4.1968.
8. *Newsweek,* 22.4.1968, quoted in O. Letelier and M. Moffitt, *The International Economic Order,* Transnational Institute, Washington (1977).
9. European Community's Press and Information, background note, 10 May 1972.
10. Comment 7, Rich v. Poor, Round 3, Christian Institute for International Relations (CIIR), London (1972) p. 1.
11. *The Times,* 22.5.1972.
12. Charter of Economic Rights and Duties of States, UN Yearbook (1974).
13. (i) The Sixth Special Session of the UN General Assembly, and the Declaration and Establishment of a New International Economic Order in 1974. (ii) The Seventh Special Session of the UN General Assembly which considered the question of development and international economic cooperation. (iii) The adoption by the General Assembly in 1974 of the Charter of Economic Rights and Duties of States. (iv) The UN Industrial Development Organisation (UNIDO) Lima Declaration and Plan of Action in 1975, which advocated a redeployment of world industrial capacity to increase the ldc share. (v) The quadrupling of oil prices by OPEC in 1973. (vi) The Conference on International Economic Cooperation, the 'North–South dialogue', begun in Paris in 1975.
14. Church Alert, UNCTAD IV, No. 7, SODEPAX, Switzerland (1976) p. 23.
15. *The tide has turned,* Report on the Fourth United Nations Conference on Trade and Development, World Development Movement (WDM) (1976).
16. *ICDA News,* 4 (1979).
17. *ODI Review,* No. 1 (1979) Table A14.
18. A. Weston, 'Review of the development scene', *ODI Review,* No. 2 (1979).
19. UNCTAD V Arusha Programme for Collective Self-reliance and Framework for Negotiations (1979).

20. ODI Briefing Paper, UNCTAD V: A Preview of the Issues No. 2 (1979).
21. *Guardian,* 10.5.1979.
22. *Hindu,* 5.6.1979.
23. *Dawn,* 6.6.1979.
24. UN Document TD 268 Add. 1 (1979).

CHAPTER 3:   THE NON-ALIGNED MOVEMENT

1. M. Gavrilovic, 'The vitality of non-alignment', *Review of International Affairs,* Vol. XXI, No. 482, Belgrade (1970).
2. W. Levi, 'The evolution of India's foreign policy', *The Yearbook of World Affairs,* Vol. 12 (1958) p. 115.
3. Text of Final Communiqué of Afro-Asian Parley, Reuters (1955).
4. V. Mendis, 'The policy of non-alignment' in 'Non-alignment and Third World solidarity', *Marga Quarterly Journal,* Colombo, Special Issue, Vol. 3. No. 3 (1976) p. 36.
5. Declaration of the heads of state or government of non-aligned countries Belgrade, Sept 1961. In 'Non-alignment and Third World solidarity', ibid., p. v.
6. *Observer,* Foreign News Service, 7.10.1964.
7. UN General Assembly, 19th Session, Document A/5763, 29.10.1964.
8. *Hindu,* 8.2.1970.
9. Ibid., 3.9.1970.
10. *Hindu,* 14.4.1970; *Observer,* Foreign News Service, 20.4.1970.
11. Quoted in 'Non-alignment and Third World solidarity', op.cit., p. xiii.
12. *Egyptian Mail,* 18.4.1970.
13. K. Kaunda, *Bank of London and South America Review,* Vol. 8 (1974).
14. Quoted in 'Non-alignment and Third World solidarity', op.cit., p. lix.
15. Ibid., p. xlvii.
16. Ibid., p. xix.
17. O. Letelier and M. Moffitt, *The International Economic Order* (Part 1), Transnational Institute, Washington (1977).
18. R. Prebisch, *Towards a New Trade Policy for Development,* Geneva, UNCTAD (1964).
19. Document A/31/1976, UN General Assembly Session, 8.9.1976.
20. Delineated in *Africa Development,* 10.10.1970.
21. 'Constitution of the non-aligned news agency pool', *India and Foreign Review,* Vol. 13, No. 20 (1976).
22. *Guardian,* 7.9.1979.
23. Ibid.
24. *Hindu,* 11.9.1979.

CHAPTER 4:   6TH AND 7TH SPECIAL SESSIONS OF THE UN

1. *Christian Science Monitor,* 5.4.1974.
2. *Financial Times,* 5.4.1974.
3. Ibid.

4. *New York Times,* 29.4.1974.
5. *Financial Times,* 16.4.1974.
6. *Guardian,* 17.4.1974.
7. Reported in *International Herald Tribune,* 23.4.1974.
8. *Financial Times,* 11.4.1974.
9. Ibid., 18.4.1974.
10. *Guardian,* 16.4.1974.
11. *New York Times,* 16.4.1974.
12. *Financial Times,* 3.5.1974.
13. *Guardian,* 3.5.1974.
14. Ibid., 2.9.1975.
15. See O. Letelier and M. Moffitt, *The International Economic Order* (Part 1), Transnational Institute, Washington (1977) p. 36.
16. *Christian Science Monitor,* 8.9.1975.
17. Ibid.
18. *New York Times,* 12.9.1975.
19. *Herald Tribune,* 6.9.1975.
20. *Financial Times,* 3.9.1975.
21. Ibid.
22. *International Herald Tribune,* 4.9.1975.
23. *New York Times,* 3.9.1975.
24. *The Times,* 17.9.1975.
25. *Financial Times,* 17.9.1975.

CHAPTER 5: OPEC

1. *Dawn,* 17.8.1960.
2. *Financial Times,* 22.8.1960.
3. Ibid., 15.9.1960. This matter was reported in only a relatively short paragraph at the time.
4. Ibid., 28.3.1963.
5. *The Times,* 8.10.1971.
6. Ibid., 25.3.1972.
7. *The Financial Times,* 19.3.1973.
8. Ibid.
9. *Guardian,* 23.3.1973.
10. *The Times,* 24.12.1973.
11. *Financial Times,* 29.1.1975.
12. Ibid., 18.12.1976.
13. *Hindu,* 9.1.1974.
14. *Financial Times,* 25.11.1975.
15. Shihata and R. Mabro, 'The OPEC aid record', *World Development,* Vol. 7 (1979), Table 1 (Net disbursement of OPEC aid 1973–7), p. 163.

CHAPTER 6: CIEC

1. *New York Times,* 11.1.1975.
2. *Egyptian Gazette,* 31.1.1975.
3. *International Herald Tribune,* 18.2.1975.
4. *Financial Times,* 8.4.1975.
5. *International Herald Tribune,* 5.4.1975.
6. 'The Paris Conference on International Economic Cooperation', ODI Briefing Paper, August (1976).
7. *The Times,* 25.4.1977.
8. *Financial Times,* 6.5.1977.
9. *Observer,* Foreign News Service, 30.5.1977.
10. Ibid.
11. *Hindu,* 1.6.1977.
12. See *Financial Times,* 3.6.1977, for further details.
13. Ibid., 4.6.1977.
14. *Guardian,* 2.6.1977.
15. 'Development cooperation: efforts and policies of the members of the Development Committee, OECD, 1978', *ODI Review,* No. 1 (1979) Table A5.
16: *The Times,* 3.6.1977.

Select Bibliography

The subject has a very extensive literature including works concerned with broad issues, documentary sources and articles from a great number of journals; in addition reports from the world's press are particularly relevant to recent events. Some detailed references have been included in the notes and what follows is a very brief selection of more comprehensive works.

M. S. Al-Otaiba, *OPEC and the Petroleum Industry* (London: Croom Helm, 1975).

G. Cunningham, *The Management of Aid Agencies* (London: Croom Helm, ODI, 1974).

T. Czentes, *The Political Economy of Underdevelopment* (Budapest: Akademiai, 1971).

E. de Kadt and G. Williams (eds). *Sociology and Development* (London: Tavistock, 1974).

P. Donaldson, *Worlds Apart: the Economic Gulf between Nations* (Harmondsworth: Penguin, 1971).

G. F. Erb and V. Kallab (eds), *Beyond Dependency: the Developing World Speaks Out* (New York: Praeger, 1975).

G. FitzGerald, *Unequal Partners* (New York: UN, 1979).

A. G. Frank, *Latin America: Underdevelopment or Revolution* (New York: Monthly Review, 1970).

B. Gozovic, *UNCTAD, Conflict and Compromise* (Leiden, Sijthoff, 1972).

P. Hallwood and S. Sinclair, *Oil, Debt and Development: OPEC in the Third World* (London: Allen and Unwin, 1981).

A. M. M. Hoogvelt, *The Sociology of Developing Societies* (London: Macmillan, 1976).

H. G. Johnson, *Economic Policies towards Less Developed Countries* (London: Unwin University Books, 1967).

A. Krassowski, *Development and the Debt Trap* (London: Croom Helm, ODI, 1974).

O. Letelier and M. Moffit, *The International Economic Order* (Part 1) (Washington: Transnational Institute, 1977).

I. Livingstone (ed.), *Economic Policy for Development* (Harmondsworth: Penguin, 1971).

P. R. Mooney, *Seeds of the Earth: a Private or Public Resource* (London: International Coalition for Development Action, 1979).

K. Morton and P. Tulloch, *Trade and Developing Countries* (London: Croom Helm, 1977).

H. Myint, *The Economics of Developing Countries* (London: Hutchinson University Library, 1967).

G. Myrdal, *Economic Theory and Underdeveloped Regions* (London: Duckworth, 1957).

C. Payer, *The Debt Trap* (Harmondsworth: Penguin, 1974).

R. I. Rhodes, *Imperialism and Underdevelopment* (New York: Monthly Review Press, 1970).

A. R. Riddell, *Restructuring British Industry: The Third World Dimension* (London: Catholic Institute for International Relations, 1979).

K. P. Sauvant and H. Hasenpflug (eds), *The New International Economic Order: Confrontation or Cooperation between North and South?* (Frankfurt: Campus Verlag, 1977).

S. Schiavo-Campo and H. Singer, *Perspectives of Economic Development* (New York: Houghton Mifflin, 1970).

R. Solomon, *The International Monetary System 1945–76* (New York: Harper & Row, 1977).

M. P. Todaro, *Economic Development in the Third World* (London: Longman, 1977).

C. K. Wilber (ed.), *The Political Economy of Development and Underdevelopment* (New York: Random House, 1973).

P. Willetts, *The Non-Aligned Movement: the Origins of a Third World Alliance* (New York: Nichols, 1978).

Index